TWAYNE'S WORLD AUTHORS SERIES

A Survey of the World's Literature

INDIA

Mohan Lal Sharma, Slippery Rock State College

EDITOR

Nirad C. Chaudhuri

TWAS 548

Nirad C. Chaudhuri

NIRAD C. CHAUDHURI

By **CHETAN KARNANI**

University of Rajasthan

TWAYNE PUBLISHERS

A DIVISION OF G. K. HALL & CO., BOSTON

Published in 1980 by Twayne Publishers,
A Division of G. K. Hall & Co.
All Rights Reserved

Printed on permanent/durable acid-free paper and bound
in the United States of America

First Printing

Frontspiece photograph of Nirad C. Chaudhuri

Library of Congress Cataloging in Publication Data

Karnani, Chetan, 1936–
Nirad C. Chaudhuri.

(Twayne's world authors series ; TWAS 548 : India)
Bibliography: pp. 135–37
Includes index.
1. Chaudhuri, Nirad C., 1897–
DS435.7.C5K37   1980   954.04′092′4   [B]
ISBN 0–8057–6245–0   78–21087

for
Ganga and Moni

Contents

About the Author

Preface

Acknowledgments

Chronology

1. A Study in Maladjustment   13

2. *The Autobiography of an Unknown Indian*   28

3. *A Passage to England*   44

4. The Hindu's European Soul   54

5. *To Live or Not to Live*   72

6. Between Tradition and Modernity   85

7. *Scholar Extraordinary*   97

8. Conclusion   112

Notes and References   127

Selected Bibliography   135

Index   138

About the Author

Chetan Karnani was born in 1936, and was educated at the Universities of Agra and Rajasthan. He got his Ph.D. on I. A. Richards under the supervision of Professor A. G. Stock. Dr. Karnani has written music and literary criticism for many Indian and foreign periodicals. His publications include: *Nissim Ezekiel* (Arnold-Heinmann, 1974) and *Listening to Hindusthani Music* (Orient Longman, 1976). His book on I. A. Richards entitled *Criticism, Aesthetics and Psychology* awaits publication in United States. Currently, Dr. Karnani is busy writing a monograph on Indo-Anglian literature at Indian Institute of Advanced Study, Simla.

Dr. Karnani's book, *Criticism, Aesthetics, and Psychology—A Study of the Writings of I. A. Richards*, was published by Arnold-Heinemann in 1977. He is an accomplished vocalist in the Kirana tradition of Hindustani music. His book, *Some Indo-English Writers—A Critical Assessment*, will shortly be published by the Indian Institute of Advanced Study, Simla.

Preface

Nirad C. Chaudhuri has been considered by some critics as India's greatest living writer of nonfictional prose in English. A brilliant polymath, with a phenomenal memory, he is distinguished as much for his abrasive style as for his provocative ideas.

Chaudhuri has to his credit as many readers in the West as in India, and indeed his most popular book is a travelogue, *A Passage to England,* which he wrote after a stay of five weeks in Great Britain. His success in the West is a result of his constant theme—modern India's encounter with the West. Few people have so persistently meditated on the East-West confrontation as Chaudhuri has, so that anyone anxious to understand contemporary India would find the study of his books indispensable.

Personally, Chaudhuri is a confused mixture of East and West. We can study this confusion in his unusually frequent self-analyses (his motto is, "Know thyself"). He has always felt an exile in India, and it is significant that in his seventies, he has chosen to become an expatriate like Henry James or Joseph Conrad, and has settled in England. There he has written the biography of the German expatriate—Max Muller—who helped enormously in the discovery of India in the nineteenth century. This latest book, *Scholar Extraordinary,* reveals Chaudhuri's exceptionally strong desire to show how familiar he is with English civilization. In the present work I have critically analyzed Chaudhuri's six books as an interesting exercise in the progressive Westernization of a unique Indian.

Chaudhuri started as an unknown Indian; he is now an almost authentic Englishman. In his first book, *The Autobiography of an Unknown Indian,* he wrote a moving indictment of British imperialism in India; in his second, *A Passage to England,* he earned a lot of cultural foreign exchange for Great Britain. He once had the courage to tell Khushwant Singh that he has not lifted his ban on the Government of India; yet the very same man had the cowardice to sell his soul to the British Council and the British Broadcasting Corporation. Moreover, he remains an inveterate anglophile despite having made a profound analysis of Indian nationalism.

This anglomania has resulted in many detractors in India. His most controversial book, *The Continent of Circe*, is particularly distasteful to Indians because the whole work is so obviously meant for foreign consumption. One can only hope that with growing national consciousness this cringing attitude toward the West—so surprising in a talented intellectual like Chaudhuri, yet so common among middle-class Indians—will become a thing of the past.

It has been my privilege to discuss a polymath like Chaudhuri with many scholars in different fields. Their interdisciplinary point of view has been a great help in the understanding of his extraordinary mind. Three scholars at the University of Rajasthan—Professor Daya Krishna of the Philosophy Department, Dr. Ram Gopal Sharma of the History Department, and Mr. A. M. Ghose of the General Education Department—gave me valuable opportunities to have many stimulating discussions with them. I am also grateful to Mr. Nissim Ezekiel, Dr. R. K. Kaul, and Mrs. Francine Krishna who read parts of the typescript and made several useful suggestions; to Mr. N. N. Gidwani, Mr. C. L. Sharma, and Mr. Vijaya Verma for their bibliographical help; to Professor Sylvia E. Bowman, Professor M. L. Sharma, and Professor V. A. Shahane for enabling me to undertake this intellectual adventure; and to Mr. L. P. Agarawal for painstaking typing of this book. Finally, I wish to express my gratitude to Mr. Nirad C. Chaudhuri himself for patiently answering my queries.

CHETAN KARNANI

University of Rajasthan,
Jaipur, India

Acknowledgments

Grateful acknowledgment is made to the following for permission to quote from the works of Nirad C. Chaudhuri: Macmillan, London and Basingstoke, for quotations from *The Autobiography of an Unknown Indian* and *A Passage to England;* Chatto and Windus, London, for quotations from *The Continent of Circe;* Chatto and Windus, London and Oxford University Press, New York for *Scholar Extraordinary;* Hind Pocket Books (P) Ltd., Delhi, for quotations from *To Live or Not to Live;* Mr. Nirad C. Chaudhuri and Associated Publishing House for quotations from *The Intellectual in India.*

I wish to thank the editor of *Quest*, Bombay, for allowing me to make use of the article on Nirad C. Chaudhuri which I originally wrote for *Quest*, No. 57, Spring 1968.

Chronology

1897 Nirad C. Chaudhuri born in Kishorganj, Myemsingh district, East Bengal (now Bangladesh), the second of eight children.

1910 Leaves Kishorganj for Calcutta.

1914 Passes matriculation examination.

1917 Writes "Objective Method in History."

1918 Graduates with a first class in History from Scottish Church College, Calcutta University.

1920 Fails exams for M.A. (History); gives up his studies.

1921 Government clerk in Military Accounts.

1924 Mother dies.

1926 Assistant editor of *The Modern Review*, under Ramanand Chatterjee.

1927 Meets poet Rabindranath Tagore.

1931 Marries his devoted wife, Amiya.

1937 Secretary to Sarat Chandra Bose.

1942 Leaves Calcutta for Delhi; appointed political commentator for All-India Radio.

1951 *The Autobiography of an Unknown Indian* published by Macmillan (London).

1955 First trip abroad to England, France, and Italy.

1959 *A Passage to England* published by Macmillan (London).

1965 *The Continent of Circe* published by Chatto and Windus (London).

1966 Duff Cooper Memorial Prize for *The Continent of Circe*.

1967 *The Intellectual in India* published by Associated Publishing House (Delhi).

1970 Leaves India for Oxford to write the life of Max Muller.

1972 Visiting professor at University of Texas and University of Chicago.

1974 *Scholar Extraordinary* published by Chatto and Windus (London).

CHAPTER 1

A Study in Maladjustment

CHAUDHURI once complained that "No intellectual effort
can be sustained on the Indian diet. Its animal protein and
vitamin content must be substantially increased."[1] While his fellow-Hindus become "semi-animate mummies"[2] after the age of
seventy, he has shown remarkable vitality at well past this age.
His faith in animal food and his Westernized habits have given
him so much energy that even in his old age he has accepted
commissions for books with various publishers. His forthcoming
works include one on the life of Clive which will trace the
development of British power in India. Currently, Chaudhuri is
busy writing a monumental book on Hinduism,[3] the study of
which has been his lifelong passion. Thus, instead of enjoying
the peace and leisure of Sanyasa Ashrama,[4] he has been busy
searching the Oxford archives to find material for his forthcoming books. He might well say, with Browning's Grammarian,
"Leave now for dogs and apes: / Man has forever."[5]

Chaudhuri's whole life has been dedicated to the pursuit of
learning, yet he was fifty-one when his first book appeared. In
his autobiography, he wanted to write off the first fifty years
of his life and begin life anew. Thus, he became a serious
author only after his retirement. Five weeks spent in England at
the invitation of the BBC inspired the anglophilic *A Passage to
England,* a book which brought him many harsh and critical
reviews in India. Chaudhuri was so angered by his Indian
critics that he determined to take revenge on all Indians. *The
Continent of Circe,* his next book, therefore takes an extreme
position in comparing Indians to pigs.

These first three books brought Chaudhuri enormous popularity
in the West. The success seems to have mellowed him, toward
his fellow-Hindus, and he has tried to make amends for his

13

former criticism of Indian society by promoting reform in
India. His collection of essays, *To Live or Not to Live* is a
brilliant analysis of social and family life in India, in which he
shows his genuine concern for the reformation of Hindu society.
His fifth work *The Intellectual in India* includes much practical
advice to Indian scholars, culled from his own experience.

In his latest work, *Scholar Extraordinary*, Chaudhuri has given
up his earlier interest in polemical writing. There is no longer
the harsh intolerance and argumentative tone that characterized
his earlier work. Thus, he seems to have arrived at a stage which
can be summed up as "Calm of mind, all passion spent."[6]

I *Early Days*

Chaudhuri wrote about his own life in great detail up to the
age of twenty-two in his autobiography. But after that he became
more interested in national than in personal history. In any case,
the man who has written his own life had better narrate it in
his own words:

I was born on Tuesday, Agrahayana 9, in the year 1304 of the
Bengali era (which corresponds to 23rd November 1897), at 6 a.m.
local time. I have no means of proving this date. I have no birth
certificate in the Western fashion, and for reasons to be given presently,
no horoscope either in the Eastern fashion. The only document in the
nature of a proof of age which I ever saw was an entry in my mother's
handwriting on the fly-leaf of her note book. But that note book has
long been lost.[7]

This whole passage is characteristic of the intimate, detailed
tone of the book. Chaudhuri is telling the reader that he cares
neither for horoscopes in the Indian fashion nor for the verifica-
tion of facts in the Western fashion. In addition, he wants to
show that he possesses an unusually sound memory.

Thus, from the outset, Chaudhuri tries to persuade the reader
that his life was different from that of other Indians. Even his
life before birth was unusual in that, while Indian parents always
talk about the expected child, his parents did not. Chaudhuri's
birth was not only unpublicized, but he was born in his father's
house. This fact is also important because other Indian families

send the expectant mother to give birth in her father's house, while Chaudhuri's father believed in a nuclear family. He thought the extended family an ill-assorted conglomeration of people without any coherence. These family circumstances show that conditions favored Chaudhuri's Westernization from his earliest days.

Chaudhuri was singularly lucky in his father. He inherited his verbal and lexicographic interest from his father, who had only an elementary education, but who drilled him in sentence patterns from his early days, and taught him, for example, the unique construction of the English verb "to have."[8] If Chaudhuri got his linguistic interests from his father, he got his interest in music from his mother. At a time when "*our* society looked upon a woman who sang as a *demi-mondaine*,"[9] his mother used to sing religious songs set to *ragas* early in the morning. Chaudhuri regrets that he did not live up to the expectations of his talented parents. His father had hoped that as a result of his individual efforts and initiative, his sons would be better placed than others, "but the peculiar genius which we the brothers developed as we grew older for spoiling our worldly prospects was the sorrow of his age and its greatest disappointment."[10]

II   *The Search for a Career*

The biggest disappointment in Chaudhuri's life was his failure to get his M.A. This was a particularly surprising setback for one who held a first class B.A. Chaudhuri got so lost in the labyrinth of learning that he read things which were not prescribed in his syllabus. Nor could his nervous system cope with the specific requirements of an Indian examination. The result was that he failed owing to "lack of vitality." It was Chaudhuri's secret ambition to be a lecturer in history but the failure in the M.A. examination shattered all his hopes of an academic career.

Chaudhuri started as a clerk in the Military Accounts Service of the Government of India in 1921. But just as Keats dreamed of Oberon and other fairies in the medical classroom, so did Chaudhuri in the Military Accounts Department: "But very soon it became disconcertingly clear to me that the kind of life the Military Accounts Department offered was impossible. I had no taste whatever for the routine work I was required to perform, and very quickly I acquired a positive dislike for it. No lure of promotion or of a better salary could put me in a frame of mind to carry on my clerical duties industriously."[11] After several months of mental agony and torture, he decided to give up the job.

After some time, he got another job as an assistant editor of the *Modern Review* at the salary of one hundred rupees a month. Even this salary was paid in meager instalments. The job gave Chaudhuri an apprenticeship in journalism, which became a lifelong interest. At present, he is one of the most sought-after contributors to India's leading periodicals. But with growing family responsibilities, Chaudhuri decided to part company with *Modern Review* after a period of five years.

Next, beginning in 1937, he worked for four years as political secretary to Sarat Chandra Bose who was a leading politician and lawyer of Calcutta. This gave Chaudhuri inside knowledge of party affairs and made him disillusioned with Indian politics. Unfortunately, his employer was arrested in 1941, which left Chaudhuri jobless once again.

At this stage, Chaudhuri's interest in military studies proved helpful. He had read articles in the *Encyclopaedia Britannica* with great interest on "artillery, ordnance, ships and ship-building."[12] So he wrote essays on military culture and history which earned him a living. Chaudhuri has said that at this time, "my financial position was so improved that when my third son was born in 1939 I used to call him Benjamin."[13] In addition to the money, his extensive knowledge of military affairs brought him testimonials from British experts such as J. C. F. Fuller and Liddell Hart.

As a result of this expert knowledge of military science, Chaudhuri got a well-paid job in the All-India Radio. He became a gazetted officer because in 1942 he was the best war commentator in the country. Also at this time, he left Calcutta and settled in Delhi. Ten years later, with the publication of his autobiography, Chaudhuri was forced to retire from the All-India Radio. He was not given a pension because he dedicated his autobiography to the memory of the British Empire in India.

Once again in need of money, Chaudhuri became an adviser

on press relations at the French Embassy. He continued with this job until 1963. Meanwhile, *A Passage to England* brought him good royalties. Thus, it is only after the age of sixty-six that Chaudhuri began working as a full-time author.

III *"Slow Rises Worth"*

Dr. Johnson's lines "This mournful truth is everywhere confess'd / Slow rises worth, by poverty depress'd"[14] apply rather well to the life of Chaudhuri. But in spite of economic hardships, he has pursued his literary ambition with unfailing vigor and has always retained his scholarly dignity: "The cultivation of important people did not come naturally to me. My life was the hermit-crab's life."[15] Without the testimonial of an influential man and without a postgraduate degree, it is difficult to get a professional-level job in India, and Chaudhuri had some difficult times because of his academic failure: "I entered the world in 1921, and for sixteen years after that suffered such poverty, want, and humiliation as I cannot wish even an enemy, if I had any, to be punished with."[16]

Long after Chaudhuri attained success as an author, he continued to mention his poverty. In *The Continent of Circe* he makes a great deal of the fact that he had to borrow a typewriter from Khushwant Singh. Matters became worse when this fact was mentioned by an American reporter in 'An Interview with Khushwant Singh" and published in the *Official Publications of the American Women's Club of Delhi*. Chaudhuri's elaborate reference to this interview only shows that he is extremely fond of publicizing his poverty. "My poverty is, of course, well known in New Delhi and much further afield, and therefore I was not prepared to see it bruited about by so august a body as the American Women's Club of Delhi."[17] Such irrelevant references only show Chaudhuri's unconscious desire for money and an official position or recognition.

It is true that poverty has deprived Chaudhuri of many things in life, but he has shown too much concern for worldly things. For instance, he regrets that he could not cultivate his hobbies because of poverty: "I have never felt happy when I have not been able to acquire a new hobby every five years, and in my hard days I did not mind my poverty overmuch as a major trial in life, but as a minor one in depriving me of hobbies."[18] Chaudhuri has not been able to lead a fuller life because of poverty, but he has remained dedicated to his vocation as an intellectual. He has mentioned desperate remedies to retain his stature as a scholar: "I cannot urge these desperate courses on others. Nor can I wish anybody to pay the price in want, suffering and humiliation that has been extorted from me."[19] But it is to his credit that he has continued to work hard under such difficult circumstances. Even without the security of a job, he has remained a dedicated intellectual.

Chaudhuri's definition of an intellectual applies to his own case. He says:

An intellectual is a man who does or tries to do the following: (1) he applies his intellectual faculties . . . to understand and interpret the world around him; (2) as a result of study, observation, and experiments he formulates conclusions which he believes to be true or, at all events, truer than those which were current before; (3) he communicates his ideas to fellowmen with a view to influencing their mind, life and actions.[20]

This definition shows that Chaudhuri is not interested in the pursuit of learning for its own sake; rather he considers it his main function to interpret his Indian environment to his readers. It is significant to note that the study of Indian history has been an imporant pursuit with Chaudhuri and that his main aim has always been to understand modern India and its encounter with the West.

IV *Interests*

Chaudhuri is a man with an exceptional zest for life. He has many hobbies which he pursues with diligence. His interests can best be described in the words of his friend V. Ramaratnam who worked with him in the All-India Radio for many years:

A keen connoisseur of Indian and Western music, Chaudhuri has a formidable collection of records of Western classical music. He is a great lover of English poetry and is never tired of entertaining his many guests with choice recitations. . . . He got interested in Western classical art early in life and his enthusiasm for it is sustained. A large part of his income is spent on books and his second floor house in old Delhi's Nicholson Road is overflowing with books on a wide variety of subjects.[21]

From his early days there was a conflict in the mind of Chaudhuri whether he should be a specialist or a "generalist." His early ambition was to fashion himself on the pattern of Leibnitz.or Goethe. With him, the key word was "synthesis." He has described his growing interest in the various branches of learning in the following words:

What I was primarily interested in even as a boy was the meaning and purpose of existence, and since existence had many facets, my intellectual interests also became many-sided. Even without my being aware of its deep springs, my appetite for information and explanation became as varied as my mental dentition became versatile. I could pass from physics to Sanskrit literature or from novels to astronomy with an agility which seemed like volatility to those who did not know me well.[22]

Chaudhuri is a formidable scholar. He spends nearly twelve hours a day reading and making notes. There are many anecdotes about his impressive range of learning, but the best description has been given by his friend Khushwant Singh, who is himself a distinguished writer. He writes:

There is little doubt that Nirad can talk on any subject under the sun. There is not a bird, tree, butterfly or insect whose name he does not know in Latin, Hindi, Sanskrit and Bengali. . . . I have heard him discuss stars with astronomers, recite lines from an obscure fifteenth century French poet to a professor of French literature, advise a wine dealer on the best vintages from Burgundy. At a small function in honour of Laxness, the Icelandic winner of the Nobel Prize for literature, I heard Nirad lecture him on Icelandic literature.[23]

This remarkable knowledge has been acquired through patient study supported by a brilliant memory. Long before Chaudhuri went to London, he knew not only where its famous museums are located, but also where the famous restaurants are located.

Chaudhuri started his literary career by writing in his mother tongue, Bengali. He has written many articles and one book in Bengali. Mr. Ramaratnam writes: "His book in Bengali *Woman in Bengali Life* is a full-length treatment of the emotional impact of the new conception of sexual relationship that appeared in Bengal in the 19th century as a result of Western influences."[24] But Chaudhuri feels that he can no longer express himself well in his mother tongue. Besides, Bengali does not have the potential to give full expression to his thoughts. The main reason he shifted to English was his desire to make a reputation in the West. This was only natural in a man who became progressively Westernized as the years passed.

Chaudhuri is keenly interested in Western music. He likes Bach and Beethoven, but his favorite composer is Mozart. He once said: "I now prefer Mozart. My granddaughter is named Papagena from *The Magic Flute*."[25] All his books have many metaphors borrowed from Western music; for example: "... the Hindu or the Muslim polygamist uses a number of women as notes in a simultaneously sounded chord, the modern Western polygamists play them *arpeggio*, making marriage very much a matter of sexual convenience."[26]

Chaudhuri also has strong feelings about food, and he has become completely Western in his eating habits, as well as his musical preference. Once he told a gathering of students of Delhi University that if they ate too much starch, they wouldn't be able to write any English better than Babu Angrezi (Indian English). It seems that his own faith in proteins allows him to write English like an Englishman.

He not only does not like Indian food, but he does not like the Indian climate either. He once said: "I, for one, never feel so fit physically as in England. I have been to England several times, and every time I return from there feeling at my physical best. I feel the depression—within weeks."[27] Since Chaudhuri feels depressed in India because of its climate, he has now settled in England.

V *Contempt for India*

As he grew increasingly Westernized, Chaudhuri increasingly treated his fellow-Indians as superstitious and boorish. In his autobiography, he tried to show that India has a lower state of civilization, compared to the West. For instance, he tried to show that Indians have a false faith in horoscopes: "The worries and complications horoscopes bring into life are almost endless to list. They draw a red herring across every personal problem—choice of profession, marriage, journeys, treatment in illness—and in truth disturb and upset every rational arrangement."[28] It is true that most Indians believe in astral congruity and that many marital alliances founder on the rock of horoscopes. R. K. Narayan depicts this fact imaginatively in *The Bachelor of Arts*.[29] But the tone of Chaudhuri's writing suggests that Indians are irrational because they believe in horoscopes.

Likewise, he tries to prove that Indians do not know anything about nutrition. He attributes all the ills of India to her poor food habits:

I am convinced that if today moral energy is lacking in India the reason is largely physical. It amounts to no more than what a nervous system sapped constantly in strength and balance by lack of sleep and solitude can generate from a sustenance of starch unrelieved by anything but a liberal sprinkling of chili. I am also convinced that by making a few but fundamental changes in our habits of food, sleep and exercise we can avoid a good deal of the evils of modern India, including the hysterical Hindu-Muslim antagonism which has succeeded in ruining our political life.[30]

This is a characteristic Chaudhuri flourish, and he is probably right when he says that the upper classes in India do not show any consciousness of the science of nutrition. But the poor, who barely maintain their existence, can hardly hope to get the proteins and vitamins which he prescribes for them.

Yet another failing of Indians, according to Chaudhuri is that they are more money-minded than any other people in the world. He would therefore have the spirituality of the people of India treated as mere window-dressing. He comes to these conclusions on the evidence of a few stray instances. For example:

Loss of sanity due to loss of money is also pretty common. At Kalikutch there was a madman, a frequent visitor at our grandmother's house, whose mental derangement had been brought about by the misappropriation of three thousand rupees by his brother. This again is a symptom of the strange duality of our lives. . . . For all that one hears about the spirituality of the people of India, while they are *in* the world they are also *of* the world, and the spell cannot be broken until it breaks itself.[31]

The generalization that Indians regard money as the world's highest and most precious gift to man is as unwarranted as Chaudhuri's generalization that Indians suffer from "didacticism and sentimentality."[32] But he is not concerned with truth here, but rather with setting up straw men so that he can claim he is different from other Indians. Now, a rich man can assert his faith in conspicuous consumption, but a poor man can hardly afford to do so. Since there is great competition for survival in India, there is a corresponding concern about money.

Chaudhuri's early education in a missionary college fostered anti-Indian attitudes toward life. As a last example of his anti-Indian bias, we could look at this period in his life and find: "It was the example of Father Prior of the Oxford Mission which first taught me that mankind could live without the protection and guarantee of padlocks. Since I saw him leaving everything about in open drawers in an open room I too gave up padlocks, and I have not been a loser."[33] In such a passage, Chaudhuri argues that Westerners have faith in mankind and Indians have not, and that he behaves like a Westerner.

The instances quoted above show that Chaudhuri had an unusual dislike for his own countrymen. They make one suspect that his autobiography was an exercise in opportunism. He has said about Indians all those things which British diehards would love to hear and put himself in the same class as the Abbé Dubois[34] and Katherine Mayo.[35]

VI   A Sensitive Man

Chaudhuri's alienation from India had been caused by the fact that he is an extremely shy, retiring sort of person. In Delhi, he had only two Indian friends, Khushwant Singh and Ruth Prawer Jhabvala. The rest of his social circle comprised only English and American friends. The more he read about English civilization, the more Westernized he became in his outlook.

Chaudhuri's vast and profound learning makes him look down on his fellow-Indians. He finds even the lives of Gandhi, Nehru, and Tagore flawed: "I have seen, come in contact with, or read about many of the highest of my countrymen—Tagore, Gandhi or Nehru. At the death of each of these men I have been terrified by the sudden onset of a conviction that their lives ended as ghastly tragedies and were not very far from that when they were living."[36] Thus, he thinks that while there was confusion between the life of thought and the life of action in the case of these great men, his own life has been one of complete dedication to his vocation as a writer and is therefore unflawed. This belief in his own rightness becomes almost megalomania at times: once, he was appointed leader of a small group; this made him so pompous that "It was almost like the young and slight Napoleon cowing down the Massénas and the Augereaus."[37]

The reason for this excessive self-importance is that Chaudhuri has never been able to adjust to his environment. He believes that he even walks in a European manner, i.e., with a sense of purpose, while his fellow-Hindus walk aimlessly. In trying to make others looks ridiculous, he himself appears quite grotesque, as in the following description: "In a Hindu environment, I have acquired the un-Hindu habit of walking in the European manner, that is to say, quickly and with a sense of goal towards which I am going. So I hear even elderly people shouting after me, 'Left, right; left, right.' Street urchins march alongside of me with long strides, and giving it up go into peals of laughter. Older boys, and occasionally even grown-ups, call out, 'Johnnie Walker!' I naturally do not seem to hear them, and walk along."[38] The best thing that Chaudhuri can do is to ignore this impertinence, but instead he makes a great fuss. By provoking such incidents and reacting to them in the way he does, he has become even more alienated from his environment.

That Chaudhuri is an extremely touchy and sensitive person can be seen from one instance which he quotes in *The Continent of Circe*. He was not allowed to sit by the side of his wife by an Anglicized lady at a concert in New Delhi. In retrospect the whole event looks like an irrelevant personal grievance, but it is magnified out of proportion.[39] Chaudhuri writes:

Never in my life in British days had any such incident happened to me. I had written that from hearsay. But that evening I was made to feel the truth of my one-time observation. Only the day before I had met Sir Malcolm Sargent, and discussed the programme with such assurance that an English lady who was near whispered to my wife, "what a bold man he is!" But after being put in my place by the (i) Anglicised, (ii) Bengali, (iii) Hindu lady, I could hardly bear to recall that conversation: it became a cankering reminiscence of my humiliation at the hands of one of the Epigoni.[40]

Instead of ignoring a minor insult, Chaudhuri makes a mountain out of a molehill. Moreover, he takes great delight in the fact that he could discuss the program with the conductor himself, which leads one to suspect that while Chaudhuri accuses Indian officials of having "English pride of class with Hindu pride of caste," he himself could be the object of the same accusation.

Chaudhuri's attacks against Indian officials may be an unconscious attempt to compensate for his early days of poverty. Also, he is only half an inch more than five feet tall, hence he subconsciously asserts himself by hitting out at the bureaucrats. In fact, he takes great pride in the fact that he is so different from them: "I take it as the highest recognition of my efficacy as a writer that the fossils in the bureaucracy and academic life call me eccentric. What should I be if I were like them."[41] An example of his dealings with these "fossils" may be seen in his reporting of an encounter with Dr. Radhakrishnan: One sentence from St. Paul in a speech by this official had made Chaudhuri comment at length: "So I rattled on, but by the time I was nearing the end of the argument I had lost all interest in it, and only noted that the man was saying, 'I know, I know,' at every pause."[42] Here, in trying to make the official look foolish, he merely makes a fool of himself; and his criticism of the bureaucratic habit of pretending to know everything fails to register because the reader feels sympathy for the hapless listener forced to endure Chaudhuri's long-winded harangue. Even when he went to England to write a book on Englishmen, he confesses ". . . when I had opportunities for meeting Englishmen, some of them very distinguished, I did not allow them to talk, but talked all the time myself."[43]

As an author, too, Chaudhuri is prolix. Thus, when asked to

reduce *The Continent of Circe* to three-fourths its original size, he had great difficulty. Originally, the life of Max Muller ran to one thousand pages, and eventually it was the publisher's editor who reduced the book to its present size.[44] Chaudhuri always acknowledges the editor's help in every book, but he complains: "... this [expression of gratitude to the publisher's editor] has been interpreted in my country, and especially by fellow-Bengalis, to mean that my books were written in the offices of the publishers by their ghosts. The risk even now exists, but I cannot allow it to frighten me from acknowledging my debts."[45]

It is because of such incidents that Chaudhuri has become completely separated from his own countrymen. He has always been a sensitive writer, lost in his own world of scholarship. This has resulted in cognitive dissonance. The more Indians have accused him of Westernization, the more uprooted he has become from his own soil.

VII *Alienation*

In his home, Chaudhuri works in Indian dress (dhoti and kurta), while he puts on his best European suit for a walk. But now his xenophilia has assumed crude forms. He keeps lamps from Holland and perfumes from Paris. He has such a dislike for things Indian that he uses only imported goods. Once he told Vijay N. Shankar and Yash Paul Narula: "I hunt for quality, you see sheer quality. See this coat, this shirt, these pants, this tie, these socks, these shoes; all from England—Bond Street—London."[46] In his craze for foreign things, he reminds one of Mrs. Mahindra[47] in *An Area of Darkness*.

This confusion in dress is evident in his mental life also. He has written in his autobiography that his friends used to chide him for devoting more time to Latin than to Sanskrit. Many Indian intellectuals suffer from similar conflicts; but Chaudhuri's interest in Western ways and ideas has completely uprooted him from his own soil. He suffers from the same ambivalence that Jawaharlal Nehru did. The latter characterized himself in the following words: "I have become a queer mixture of the East and West, out of place everywhere, at home nowhere. Perhaps my thoughts and approach to life are more akin to what is called

Western than Eastern, but India clings to me as she does to all her children, in innumerable ways; and behind me lie, somewhere in the subconscious, racial memories of a hundred generations of Brahmins."[48] Like the first prime minister of India, Chaudhuri has inherited the collective unconscious of an Indian, but he is no less Westernized than was Nehru in the early and middle phase of his life.

This maladjustment is evident in Chaudhuri's autobiography. He asserts that he does not care for his environment because he is self-contained. He provides a fine instance of a scholar's isolation from his surroundings. Thus he can say: "I have not uprooted myself from the native soil by sojourn in a foreign country or by foreign schooling; I have only to look within myself and contemplate my life to discover India; my intellect has indeed at last emancipated itself from my country."[49] In psychological terms, this could be called schizophrenia.

This ambivalent attitude toward India can be seen in his attitude to England also. Chaudhuri dedicated his autobiography "to the memory of the British Empire in India which imposed slavery upon us." This was the debit side. The credit side of the British rule was that "all that was best in us was made, shaped and quickened." This tension is maintained throughout the first book in the form of the imagined England of literature and painting and the real England of soldiers and bureaucrats who managed the British Empire in India.

Another reason for Chaudhuri's alienation is the difference between his early and later environment. In the village of his early childhood, he was a part of his environment. He belonged to Kishorganj. But once he moved to a big city like Calcutta, the sense of social inferiority and intellectual superiority led to the following: "In relation to modern Indian society I am like an aeroplane in relation to the earth. It can never rise so high as to be able to sever its terrestrial connexion, but its flight enables it to obtain a better view of the lie of the land."[50] In short, Chaudhuri tried to study the whole of Indian society in relation to himself. It is for this reason that in his autobiography, he swerves between description of his own life and that of the history of his country.

It is no surprise that the only job that suited the temperament of Chaudhuri was that of a journalist "who is as ready as his paper to circulate everywhere for a penny and bear gladly on his back any advertisement he is paid for."[51] Thus he has become "a nomad of the industrial age," wandering from place to place in search of employment. It is significant to note that Chaudhuri has spent his last eight years in England and America.

The alienation has grown with the years. Chaudhuri has himself traced the growth of this phenomenon in the following words: "During the years of my education I was becoming a stranger to the environment and organizing my intellectual and moral life on an independent nexus; in the next ten years I was oppressed by a feeling of antagonism to the environment; and in the last phase, I became hostile to it."[52] This progressive alienation can be attributed to the fact that the more Chaudhuri has been disillusioned with India, the more he has adored the England of his romantic imagination. Yet another reason for his alienation is the fact that while Chaudhuri has developed a highly rationalistic and skeptical attitude toward the Indian way of life, he has been highly idealistic about the Western way of life. Mr. M. Naimuddin Siddiqui rightly points out: "The discipline of cultural xenogamy seems to be rigorous and needs the maintenance of an equality of status in the two partners. It is here that Mr. Chaudhuri's cultural code has failed him. His indictment of his own culture and attachment to the European culture make this only too obvious."[53]

Chaudhuri has never been able to reconcile himself emotionally to India. He could resolve the problem of his alienation only on the intellectual level. He has himself analyzed the genesis and growth of his maladjustment in the following words: "The process was simply this: that while I was being carried along by the momentum of our history, most of my countrymen were being dragged backwards by its inertia. We had been travelling in opposite directions, and are still doing so."[54]

CHAPTER 2

The Autobiography of an Unknown Indian

CHAUDHURI'S autobiography is a difficult book to summarize, for its scope is wide. It is at once history, anthropology, political science, sociology, Indology, genetics, and perhaps other disciplines. He says explicitly that "this book is ... more of a national than personal history" (p. 465).[1] In fact a careful study of Chaudhuri's book shows that he is interested more in cultural anthropology than in himself and it was his hope that the book would be a contribution to contemporary history, which indeed it is. It is interesting to note that the fourth section of the autobiography is devoted entirely to the analysis of the politics, culture, and history of India.

In the book, Chaudhuri describes his life up to the age of twenty-two, and the rest of the book contains an analysis of the Hindu way of life. The whole work might be said to have the structure of a symphony—a collection of various themes with development and recapitulation. The book begins as a description of the East Bengal landscape, passes into the early life of the author, then goes on to the general description of the entire nation. It runs to more than 500 pages, and there is every reason to suspect that Macmillan did not ask Chaudhuri to reduce the length because it contains a lot of material which earned much-needed goodwill for the British—the erstwhile rulers of India. For instance, he says that "India had no viceroy of genius after Lord Curzon. Hardinge, Reading, and Willingdon were clever men who succeeded in stealing a few marches on the nationalists" (p. 320). After this balanced judgment, he goes on to say that he wanted Winston Churchill to be sent as viceroy to India, because Churchill did not want to preside over the liquidation of the British Empire in India. Chaudhuri's admiration for Churchill

28

us feel that this Muslim festival was half a purely human activity
and half the activity of something transcending both man and
the earth altogether" (p. 35).

Among other festivals, the most brilliant description is that of
Durga Puja—the most important festival of Bengal. This annual
festival which takes place in October at the turn of the seasons
is associated with dance and music. Chaudhuri provides a brilliant
explanation of the genesis of this festival.

As we performed it there was in the ritual the idea of a beneficent
mother goddess, as well as of a destructive mother goddess, the idea
of a daughter separated from her mother and rejoined to her only for
three days in a very human sense and not in the more esoteric sense of
Persephone coming back to Demeter, the idea of a martial ritual held
on the eve of a campaign, the idea of a goddess of the lower world
demanding the blood of certain animals and conferring strength on
her worshippers in return, and along with it, the idea of the more
sunny sacrifice of the Aryan peoples, shared alike by the Hindu, the
Greek, and the Roman, which even a Christian Pater and Christian
Keats could partly understand and partly wonder at. (pp. 63–64)

It is at this festival that goats and buffaloes are sacrificed to
appease the wrathful goddess. Chaudhuri's pictorial description
of this sacrifice is obviously given for the benefit of his foreign
readers. He treats India as if it were a sort of anthropological
showpiece. Yet, as a nostalgic description of East Bengal, the
early environment provides a thrilling start to Chaudhuri's
autobiography.

II *Chaudhuri's England*

Commenting on the success of his second book, *A Passage to
England,* Chaudhuri wrote: "this success has been due to a
special and, one might even say, an accidental factor—the curious
emotional relationship between me and England from childhood."[3] Long before Chaudhuri went to England, he had formed
many boyish notions about the place. England formed a part
of his early mental environment. For this reason, in his autobiography he explains: "'. . . as England, evoked by imagination
and enjoyed emotionally, has been as great an influence on me

as any of the three places, sensibly experienced, I shall add a fourth chapter to complete the description of the early environment of my life" (p. 3).

England had such a hold on his imagination that he compares Kishorganj to an English country town: "The place had nothing of the English country town about it, if I am to judge by the illustrations I have seen and the descriptions I have read, these being my only sources of knowledge" (p. 4). Of course, in his early days, England was a disturbing presence all the time, and Chaudhuri expressing his boyish wonder, says that "the chiaroscuro of our knowledge of England was extremely sensational" (p. 99). This came from the fact that the growth of his intellectual relationship with England was rather slow. He goes on to catalogue the names of English and European personalities with which he was familiar. The first group includes Queen Victoria, Prince Albert, Napoleon, Shakespeare, and Raphael. The next group comprises Milton, Burke, Warren Hastings, Wellington, King Edward VII and Queen Alexandra. According to Chaudhuri, these personalities belonged to the proto-memorial age and "these ideas and associations constituted what I may describe as the original capital of our intellectual and spiritual traffic with the West" (p. 100).

It is an interesting exercise in the cross-fertilization of ideas that Chaudhuri reads Indian notions into European personalities. Thus, King Edward VII was only "an elderly boy" because he was never taken seriously by his mother. On the other hand, Queen Alexandra is treated in terms of the Indian relationship of "a daughter-in-law baiting mother-in-law." Homer was treated as the joint father of poetry along with Valmiki, the legendary author of the Sanskrit *Ramayana*. Milton was known not only because he was the champion of liberty but because he was the model for the Bengali epic poet Michael Madhusudhan Dutt.

Like most Indians, the things that Chaudhuri liked most about English civilization were cricket and poetry. In his early days, he liked Tennyson's "Break, Break, Break" and Wordsworth's "The earth has not any thing to show more fair." About the latter, he feels that when he read the first six lines, "the heavenly light of dawn with its purity and peace seemed to descend on us." (p. 114). It was the study of English poetry which enabled

Chaudhuri to visualize England as half land and half sea. He refers to Shakespeare's sea dirge, "Full fathom five thy father lies" side by side with Webster's land dirge, "Call for the robin-red-breast and the wren." Both poems evoke a fine pattern of England as half land and half sea.

Ignorance about Englishmen in the flesh existed side by side with an ambivalent attitude toward them. There was an irrational cringing accompanied by an unconquerable hatred. Even Mahatma Gandhi was not free from this combination of servility and malice. Once, after praising Nehru as a "Harrow boy" and "Cambridge undergraduate," Gandhi went on to declare, "our future presidents will not be required to know English" (p. 117). Gandhi's ambivalence can be seen in Chaudhuri also, even though he claims that he treats English gentlemen as English gentlemen, nothing less, nothing more. Whatever Chaudhuri's attitude toward Englishmen might be, his attitude toward Englishwomen is anything but servile. It seems that he tends to relax [his dignity] in the presence of Englishwomen. Thus, when he saw one Mrs. Nathan for the first time, he remembered "her blue eyes, her flaxen hair, her dress and her hat for the whole day" (p. 118). He was so impressed that he makes the following pronouncement: "It was many years before I had a second opportunity of seeing an Englishwoman at the same close range. But the thorough examination I had made at the very first opportunity carried me well through the barren intervening years" (p. 119).

Chaudhuri suffers from the same weakness for white skin that most other Indians do. But even in the case of the white skin, the love-hate relationship toward Englishmen persists. While they are admired for their white color, there are many curious notions about the cause of their white skin. For instance, it has been believed that immediately after their birth English babies were thrown into a tub filled with wine which bleached their skin white; or it was believed that they were white because they suffered from a skin disease like leprosy. Thus, the Hindus took revenge on Englishmen by calling them *mlechcha* or unclean foreigners. This fact makes Chaudhuri so angry that he writes about his fellow-Hindu: "He is intolerably humiliated, and in his unforgiving envy and hatred he seeks to obliterate the foreigner's superiority by casting on it the shame of the most loathsome disease which can afflict a man" (p. 126). The tone of this sentence clearly shows how anxious Chaudhuri is to defend the white-skinned foreigners.

In any case, Chaudhuri's autobiography is a valuable record of Indian attitudes toward Englishmen. It recalls those days of the British Raj when Englishmen were treated with fear and envy in India. As a chronicle of days gone by, it is a useful guide to any future historian. Mr. K. Raghavendra Rao has rightly said: "One of the greatest achievements of the *Autobiography* is to study Imperialism as a cultural problem. It shows how complex, confusing and even ridiculous can be the human drama involved in Empire-building, Empire-running and Empire-dismantling!"[4] It is significant that Chaudhuri started writing his book only after India attained freedom. It remains a brilliant epitaph on British rule in India.

III   *Indian Renaissance*

One of the main themes of Chaudhuri's autobiography is that Indian life was "made, shaped and quickened" by British rule. Thus the Indian Renaissance, which started in the nineteenth century, aspired for the synthesis of the best in India and Europe. It started with the founding of the famous Hindu college in 1817. Raja Rammohan Roy was the first person to express the new moral, religious, literary, and humanistic ideals. As a result of his pioneering efforts, many Bengalis embraced Christianity because they thought that religion was the secret of the West's superiority. The finest fusion of the East and the West perhaps took place in the case of Michael Madhusudhan Dutt who based his epic in Bengali on the models of Homer, Virgil, Dante, Tasso, and Milton.

It is Chaudhuri's thesis that even the discovery of ancient India was the work of Western orientalists. He goes to extremes and writes that civilization in India is "the provincial edition of the civilization of Europe" (p. 461). To prove his point, he distorts facts. For instance, so far as the discovery of the Vedas is concerned, he gives more credit to Max Muller than to Dayanand Saraswati; he lays greater stress on the Brahmo Samaj which was influenced by Christianity than on the Arya Samaj which revived orthodox Hinduism. Moreover, even ancient Indian culture, according to Chaudhuri, is not the basis for the Hindu culture of his day: "They [the Hindus] were being as imitative when copying ancient Indian ways as they were in copying the Western" (p. 456). There is some truth in this statement, which can be corroborated with an example from Indian music. Most people believe that Pandit V. N. Bhatkande was responsible for the revival of Indian music, but it is surprising that Bhatkande, who had the entire Sanskrit musicology at his disposal, chooses to quote Western experts on Indian music like William Jones, Augustus Willard, E. E. Clements and F. H. Fox-Strangeways.

So far as religion was concerned, Bankim Chandra Chatterjee and Vivekananda tried to explain Hinduism in the new rationalistic terms of the West. Some orthodox Hindus had come to believe that "every Hindu custom and every Hindu taboo found its justification in some theory of electricity or magnetism. At times even the science of bacteriology, new at the time, was invoked" (p. 203). Chaudhuri dismisses all of this as mumbo-jumbo and points out that revitalization of Hinduism could not have been possible if the new Western norms had not been applied to it.

The Indian Renaissance also brought a new morality. Chaudhuri notes that in his early days he was supposed to write in his diary about his "infatuation with female beauty." This puritanical record of erotic longings was a denial of human instincts. It is an example of the orthodox rigor against which Chaudhuri argues: "Thus to ask an Indian to be balanced among a number of things, each good in its way, is to ask him, not to be effective in his varied loyalties, but to be futile in all of them. He has neither the vitality nor the will power which springs from that vitality to observe proportion in his pursuits" (pp. 216–17). This new love of vitality could not have come if Brahmoism had not been "an application of Christianity to Hinduism." Thus Chaudhuri grew up in an atmosphere of moral awareness in which Christian-European ethics was in constant tension with the Hindu view of morality. This fascinating confrontation is the main theme of his autobiography.

IV *Indian Nationalism*

Chaudhuri's autobiography is a valuable addition to the study of Indian nationalism. It is record of the feelings of a sensitive man who could not reconcile himself to the idea of foreign domination. Chaudhuri recalls the fact that he used to adore the revolver as something that could help him get rid of the British; and once, his brother broke a jug because he thought it a foreign article, a symbol of alien rule. Chaudhuri's attitude toward Indian nationalism is pithily summed up in the following sentence: "We knew that our present condition was pitiable: we were poor, subjugated and oppressed, and even degenerate in certain respects; but we knew that we were great once and should be even greater in the future" (pp. 224–25). While other ancient civilizations had declined, Indian civilization alone had the capacity to rejuvenate itself. With this as his fond dream, Chaudhuri believed in republicanism and read the history of the freedom movements of other countries. Patriotic songs provided the required inspiration for nationalism. The theme of these songs invariably was that Hindu civilization should regain its pristine glory.

Although Chaudhuri passionately wanted India free he did not think the British delayed the declaration of independence by exploiting Hindu-Muslim enmity. "Heaven preserve me from the dishonesty, so general among Indians, of attributing this [Hindu-Muslim] conflict to British rule, however much the foreign rulers might have profited by it. Indeed they would have been excusable only as gods, and not as man the political animal, had they made no use of the weapon so assiduously manufactured by us, and by us also put into their hands. But even then they did not make use of it to the extent they might easily have done" (p. 229). Here, the facts of history don't bear Chaudhuri out: The two-nation theory came to be formulated during the British days. Chaudhuri himself admits that the compartmentalization of the two communities started first in education, then in politics.

One purpose of Chaudhuri's autobiography is to explode the view that Indian nationalism started in the twentieth century and that it was imported from the West. He demolishes this misconception by saying that the great Muslim scholar, Alberuni, was the first person to note Indian nationalism in the latter part of the tenth century. Chaudhuri finds the genesis of Indian nationalism in Alberuni's well-known statement: "The Hindus believe that there is no country but theirs, no nation like theirs, no science like theirs. They are haughty, foolishly vain, self-conceited and stolid." Chaudhuri agrees with Alberuni and believes that the Hindus hated all foreigners. Thus, they remained separate from the Muslims, who easily conquered a people whose fatalism made them so weak. The best feature of Chaudhuri's autobiography is that a Hindu has explained from inside what other Hindus might have felt. He rightly says that the prolonged period of subjection made the Hindus hate-addicts. At first, their hatred was fixed upon Muslims; subsequently it was transferred to the British.

Chaudhuri is very critical of Mahatma Gandhi's contribution to Indian nationalism. He believes that Gandhism appealed to the masses because it simplified all moral issues. From this point of view, Chaudhuri believes that Gandhism was not only irrational but anti-rational: "Gandhism in its rejection of civilization and reason was in one sense a descent towards the old rancorous and atavistic form of Indian nationalism" (p. 440). Mr. Richard Lannoy, in his brilliant book on India, makes a similar point when he says: "In comparison with Vivekananda, Aurobindo, Tilak, Tagore, and Nehru, the autodidact Gandhi is an untutored man of the people."[5] But Chaudhuri goes to extremes in his indictment of Gandhi when he says: "The good that he was perished at the hands of the Evil he had helped to triumph" (p. 442). Chaudhuri blames Gandhi for riots and student demonstrations, which are frequent occurrences in India now.[6]

These earlier views of Chaudhuri can be better understood by putting them side by side with his views expressed in a recent article.[7] In the twentieth century, Indian nationalism has undergone various fluctuations. In order to get rid of British rule, various generations adopted different forms of non-cooperation. As Chaudhuri puts it: "These alternations of enthusiasm and depression produced a crescendo of hatred and emotional revulsion from British rule without any hope of removing it, and

made nationalism more and more negative."[8] Indians attributed
their poverty to British rule. Thus, the course of Indian foreign
policy was determined by hatred for British rule. It is against
this background that free India has been pro-Arab and anti-Israel.
Likewise, Chaudhuri regards India's friendship with the Soviet
Union as a corollary of anti-British and anti-Western feeling.
From this point of view, he goes on to consider Indian nationalism in terms of persistent East-West dichotomy:

... the ancient East-West conflict is continuing in a new and em-
bittered form. Beginning with the wars between the Greeks and the
Persians, it ran its course through the wars between Christianity and
Islam, and it is not less of an historical fact today. In its essence it is
a conflict between the successive forms of Western civilisation from
the Hellenic to the American on the one hand, and all the parallel
non-Western civilisations on the other.[9]

V *Contemporary Indian History*

Chaudhuri said explicitly: "My main intention is thus historical,
and since I have written the account with the utmost honesty
and accuracy of which I am capable, the intention in my mind
has become mingled with the aspiration that the book may be
regarded as a contribution to contemporary history" (p. vii).
Since his life runs parallel to India's freedom struggle, one who
is interested in the story of India's freedom will find his autobiography indispensable.

Chaudhuri's autobiography recalls the painful days when
Indians first became aware that they were treated as second-
class citizens in their own county. He describes the Indian attitude toward the British Government: "The common people
still called it the Company, others Queen Victoria, and the educated the Government. The feeling, thus ever present, of a
watching and protecting Government above us vanished at one
stroke with the coming of the nationalist agitation in 1905. After
that we thought of the Government, in so far as we thought of it in
the abstract, as an agency of oppression and usurpation" (p. 48).
The book is a faithful record of oppression and persecution
during the British rule. He recalls that his brother was not allowed to go abroad because he was suspect in the eyes of the

police. In another case, when a guest came to his house in Kishorganj, the police took him to be a revolutionary. Chaudhuri impolitely asked his guest to leave earlier than he had planned to. The text has the comment: "Our oriental standards of hospitality had withered sadly under the shadow of police persecution" (p. 327). As a final example, Chaudhuri was so sensitive that he could not eat after he heard about General Dyer's massacre in Amritsar.

VI A Theory of History

Chaudhuri is not only fond of musing on Indian history but has his own theory of history in general. He is a firm believer in the "objective method in history." He has published an essay on that subject in his autobiography—an essay he wrote as an undergraduate, which he continues to believe. He has such an unshakable faith in historical integrity that he does not allow his patriotism to overpower historical considerations. At a time when history was made to serve the cause of India's freedom, Chaudhuri had the courage to write: "When most of my fellow-students and teachers appeared to think that history existed only for the sake of exalting Indian nationalism, I with all my love for my country came to regard a lapse from historical rectitude as even more condemnable than a lapse from moral conduct" (p. 342). This statement is true perhaps only in theory. In fact, Chaudhuri has interpreted Indian history from the British point of view.

Chaudhuri took Lord Acton as his model historian. He hates the subjective approach to history which emphasizes opinions and not facts. Since he has given an elaborate youthful testament of his objective approach, this might well be quoted in his own words:

The contrast of this is the objective method; it is in a word the dogma of impartiality. But this impartiality has a deeper meaning than what we understand the word to denote. To an ordinary man it means no more than justice. . . . But the objective method does not conceive of judging to be the true vocation of history, and from grounds moral as well as historical. It may be asked by what standards are we to judge bygone events and men; how are we to guage their comparative merits

and demerits? We may take our stand on the newest ideal and the
most advanced position, but these ideals are a matter of historical
growth. . . . The historian must be content to state facts as they
happened, or, to use a modern phrase, to show a development, without intruding his opinions and predilections into the narrative.
(pp. 345–46)

In other words, the objective historian cares only for ascertained
truth and whole facts and eliminates his personal attitudes as
far as possible. For instance, in describing the caste system
in ancient India, the historian can only say these were the conditions that gave rise to that system and these were the needs it
satisfied. Beyond this, every other statement falls beyond the
purview of the objective historian. In other words, history should
be above personal prejudices and national interests.

This is a laudable aim but impossible to put into practice.
No sensible historian any longer believes totally in Lord Acton
and his "objectivity." In so far as the historian sees the past
in terms of the present, he cannot ignore value judgments. Gibbon
was surprised to find that even about a street quarrel there were
so many different versions; he could not ascertain the full facts.
Croce said that all history is "contemporary history," while Collingwood believed that "history is the re-enactment in the historian's mind of the thought whose history he is studying."[10]
Nevertheless, Chaudhuri continues to believe in his earlier essay.

The truth is that if the historian cares only for the bare facts,
then he becomes a mere compiler or chronicler. Mr. Rajiva Deva
points out the problem:

The fundamental assumption of the purity of facts, on which the
objective school rests, is an impossibility. Facts are either distorted
on record by the wishes of statesmen, or else become historical facts
by virtue of their acceptance by the historian. Contemporary documents
are written by individuals, often individuals belonging to a narrow
class. History, however, is the history of whole societies, or at least
of individuals in society, seen in perspective. So, behind the two-
dimensional record of the past, we must see the three-dimensional
reality. To expect the historian to eliminate completely the distortions
existing in his material is like crying for the moon.[11]

Recently, a more balanced view has been provided by E. H.
Carr who says: "History is a continuous process of inter-action

between the historian and his facts, an unending dialogue between the past and the present."[12] Such a view points out the limitations of the objective method. When Chaudhuri says that he has not given up his early faith in his objective method, he perhaps shows that he has not kept abreast of twentieth century trends in the philosophy of history.

VII   *A Version of Indian History*

Chaudhuri's reading of Indian history is as simplistic as his theory of history. He wants to reduce Indian history to a rigid pattern. Hence the entire course of Indian history is neatly pigeonholed into three cycles. According to Chaudhuri, the first period of Indian history starts from an unknown age to A.D. 1192, when Muhammad Ghauri defeated Prithviraj. The second period of Indian history began in A.D. 1192 and continued till A.D. 1757, when the British won the battle of Plassey. From then on, the third period of Indian history started, and this period is still continuing. Chaudhuri conveniently labels these three periods as Hindu, Muhammadan, and British. Ethnically, these three cycles correspond to Indo-Aryan, Indo-Turkish and Indo-British phases of Indian history.

According to Chaudhuri, the dominant languages in these three periods were Sanskrit, Persian, and English respectively. Thus, he supplements the ethnic criterion with the linguistic one. As he puts it: "In the first cycle India used Sanskrit (with the Prakrits), in the second Persion (with the new Indian vernaculars), and in the third English (with the modern Indian languages)" (p. 473). The fact that this is only a convenient generalization can be seen from the way in which a well-known historian, Professor A. K. Majumdar, refutes Chaudhuri's thesis. Professor Majumdar writes: "Mr. Chaudhuri's belief that Persian replaced Sanskrit betrays his ignorance of history as well as of Indian phliosophy. . . . If not most, at least a major part of the standard works on Indian philosophy written in Sanskrit were the products of this period. All the modern north Indian languages took shape during this period. Their affinity is with Sanskrit, not with Persian. Major works of Hindu religious literature like the *Ramayana* of Tulasidas and Krittivasa were composed in this period."[13]

Chaudhuri's version of Indian history is not only naive and simplified, it is extremely pessimistic. He goes to great extremes when he says: "There is as yet very inadequate realisation of the fact that civilisations in the successive historical cycles in India are foreign importations" (p. 478). He even says that Hindus are foreigners in India.[14] He believes that the Indians have periodically rejuvenated themselves through foreign influences. Initially, Indian civilization arose from the impact of Aryans on the autochthons; in the second phase, it was the Muslim influence that gave new life to the local peoople; while in the third phase, the European influence is still continuing. As a result of the second phase of Indian history, Urdu words still have precedence over Sanskrit words in the vocabulary of North Indians. While, as a result of the third phase of Indian history, English words are predominant in the thinking of even the Indians of the lower classes. Chaudhuri believes that the influence of English has changed the syntax of Indian languages and that the development of prose in most Indian languages during the nineteenth century was entirely due to English influence. He concludes: "The linguistic basis of modern Indian culture, which is made up of a combination of English, a denatured written vernacular, and a mixed colloquial language, is the first proof of the essentially foreign character of modern Indian culture" (p. 486).

There is no doubt that Chaudhuri gives his version of Indian history in the form of an easily comprehensible pattern for the benefit of foreigners. In so doing, he excludes all those elements of Indian history which do not suit his design or his talents. Thus he says that since he knows nothing about the Dravidians, he rejects the idea of Dravidian influence on Hindu civilization (p. 479). This omission only demonstrates that Chaudhuri is just not interested in the history of South India. Professor A. K. Majumdar points out another significant omission in his simplistic view of Indian history: "One looks in vain in his works for any discussion of the Harappa culture. The distribution of Harappa sites discovered so far show that the area included in the perimeter connecting the outermost sites would be about half a million square miles. It appears that Mr. Chaudhuri has dismissed this great urban culture as contemptuously as economics, probably because it does not fit in with his theory that all civilisations in India are imported."[15]

Chaudhuri proves India's dependence on the West by showing that all great men in India initially got their recognition in the West. Neither Rammohan Roy nor Rabindra Nath Tagore was accepted by his countrymen until they were first honored in the West. Swami Vivekananda traveled for twelve years all over India, finding no way to work for his countrymen; so he went to America. He was received in India as an eminent thinker only when the parliament of religions at Chicago gave him an unusually warm welcome. S. Chandrashekhar, an eminent astrophysicist, settled in the U.S.A. so that he could pursue his research. Har Gobind Khorana got his Nobel Prize as an Indian, but all his work was done in America. Even Chaudhuri got recognition in India only when his autobiography was published in London. Overnight, he became a well-known Indian.

The reason for foreign dominance in India, according to Chaudhuri, is that Hindus are docile. While Indians accepted foreign rulers passively, these foreign rulers never adjusted themselves to the Indian environment. Chaudhuri's faith in climatology, vehemently expressed in *The Continent of Circe*, is first formulated in the autobiography. He calls the Indo-Gangetic plain "the Vampire of geography, which sucks out all creative energy and leaves its victims as listless shadows" (p. 502). Thus, Indian climate, physiography, and diet combine to create insipidity in the form of "dullness of the mind, monotony of experience, and narrowness of interests" (pp. 502–03). India's poor performance in the Olympic games only proves this theory. Besides, India's mediocre standards in science, literature, and technology are in keeping with his gloomy view of Indian life.

All these facts cause Chaudhuri to predict that in the days to come America will provide the new stimulus for Indian civilization: "I expect either the United States singly or a combination of the United States and the British Commonwealth to re-establish and rejuvenate the foreign domination of India" (p. 507). America is already a force to reckon with in the cultural life of India. Chaudhuri's prophetic utterance may not prove true in the political field but it certainly has done so already in the cultural field.

CHAPTER 3

A Passage to England

IN 1955, Chaudhuri went to England for five weeks to give talks for the overseas service of the B.B.C. He had already mentally lived in England from his early days. This first visit evoked such "sensations sweet,/Felt in the blood, and felt along the heart"[1] that he became lyrical about every aspect of English life. He was determined not only to compare Hindu society unfavorably with a Western one but also to praise everything English. It comes as no surprise, therefore, that he found peace and happiness in Europe. His personality underwent such a transformation in England that he expresses a secret exultation toward the end of *A Passage to England* when an Englishman working in Calcutta told him that he did not look like a Bengali (p. 229). It is surprising that he failed to see the ironical overtone in the Englishman's remark. It seems that England cast such a spell on him that he was willing to give up his roots. Yet in spite of his Anglo-Saxon virtues Chaudhuri is not free from oriental lethargy.

In his book *A Passage to England* he offers an odd apology to an English lady whose letter failed to get any response from him. He rationalizes his idleness in the following words: "East of Suez we disregard the commandment about replying to letters, but I hope that if the lady who wrote the letter sees these lines she will accept my apologies" (p. 149).

In keeping with the ambivalent personality of its author, *A Passage to England* is an unusual travelogue. V. S. Naipaul, Dom Moraes, and Ved Mehta, in their Indian travelogues describe the scents and sounds and the local color of the country. Chaudhuri does not get lost in his immediate surroundings in his book on England. Instead, there is always the basic assumption that England is different from India. He himself says explicitly: "In

44

fact, I do not think I had any conscious theory at all: my senses worked below the conscious level in such a manner that one-half of my perception of England was the perception of something *not-India.* I saw things there in doublets—there were the things which were positively English, but there were also their shadows cast in a dark mass under the light from India" (p. 3). It is for this reason that his book is as much a passage to India as to England. It is a variation on Chaudhuri's favorite theme—the contrast between the East and the West. Mr. C. Paul Verghese remarks: "It is perhaps this fact of East-West confrontation in his mind that made him call his book *A Passage to England* after E. M. Forster's famous novel *A Passage to India.*"[2]

With his interest in English literature, European art, and Western music, Chaudhuri was able to revive these sensations in the real physical environment which he had earlier experienced only in his imagination. His book can best be described in terms of the heading of one of his chapters: "The Adventures of a Brown man in Search of Civilisation." It was unfortunate that he chose to see England against the background of India. His visit only confirmed his deep-set bias against his own country. The result was a certain brooding on differences, for instance: "Time has made the face of my country stark, chastened, and sad, and it remains so in spite of the lipstick that is being put on it by the hand of the spiritual half-castes. The face of England remains smiling" (p. 7).

I *The English Scene*

It is characteristic of Chaudhuri's salesmanship that he started his book on England with a Hindu belief in rebirth. He believes that Hindus love money because they feel that they will continue to use it in their after-life. He writes: "We [Hindus] deny ourselves every comfort, contemptuously rejecting the Western notion of improving the standard of living, in order to lay by and leave a fortune at death, so that we may not be poor in future birth" (p. 12). In other words, Indians can expect a welfare state like the one enjoyed in England only in their life-after-death. Paradoxically the Hindus believe that this world is an illusion, yet they continue to cling to mundane things.

Like many other Indians Chaudhuri knew his Cumner Hills and Bablock Hythe through the study of Matthew Arnold. He says: "English literature is the best guide for foreigners to the English scene because it is more closely the product of its geographical environment, more ecological, than any other literature I have read. I think English literature has gone farthest in fusing Nature and the spirit of man" (p. 15). He had an unusual liking not only for English places but also for English characters in fiction and in real life. Such is his zest for P. G. Wodehouse that he says: "If I am to be anything of an Englishman at all, I would rather be an imitation of Jeeves, the manservant, than of his gentleman master" (p. 16).

Chaudhuri was so impressed by English gardens that they appeared to him "three-dimensional." He attributes this effect to variations of level: "Until I had seen them with their terraces, sunk lawns, ponds and hedges, I could never imagine that gardens could be so architectural and even statuesque" (p. 22). From this fact, Chaudhuri goes on to argue that oriental art is linear whereas Western art is plastic, because "the different forms of art simply reflect the different appearances" (p. 23). Even as regards perception, Chaudhuri finds a difference between the East and the West, which he describes in the following terms: "We see the world as it dictates our way of seeing, we in the East in one, a *rarefied* way, and they in the West in another, a *concrete* way" (p. 24).

The influence of climate on human behavior is the theme which appears repeatedly in Chaudhuri's first three books. In the nineteenth century, B. M. Malabari, who was proud to be an Indian even during the country's colonial days, noticed the influence of climate on the temperament of the English. Malabari writes: 'The climate of a country reflects itself pretty clearly in the temper, habits and general surroundings of the people. This is a scientific truth, the force of which is brought home to my rude intelligence most vividly in England. The people seem to be as changeable and restless as the weather. They are always on the move. . . . In a word the Englishmen seem to be as fickle as their weather."[3] Like Malabari, Chaudhuri is so obsessed with the idea of climate, that he regards it as the most important factor which distinguishes the East from the West. As he puts it:

"What divides the East from the West is neither Anglo-Saxon pride nor Hindu xenophobia. Both have indeed done their worst, but even they could not have made the division so unbridgeable without a contribution from something infinitely stronger, something which is absolutely basic to man's existence on earth—temperature" (p. 26). He feels that because of the difference of temperature, man has to wage a relentless battle against nature in the East. He says: "In the East, man is either a parasite on Nature or her victim, here [in the West] man and Nature have got together to create something in common" (p. 28).

Ten years later, Chaudhuri's second visit to England inspired him to write an article entitled "Indian England," which he wrote for *The London Magazine.* Here, he continues to express his love for England with unabated vigor. A few passages from the romantic poets inspire the following lines: "There is a distinct sensation that the writer is crossing the boundary lines between the world of senses and the world of mysticism. The characteristic quality of these passages appears to have been called forth by the *mystique* of the English scene."[4] Chaudhuri found this supra-human quality not only in Wordsworth and Keats but also in Constable and Turner. He is so fascinated by the English scene that he says: "The matter of fact reason is that the English countryside has solitude, whereas the Indian has only emptiness."[5]

II *The English People*

Chaudhuri's description of the English people is highly flattering to them. Except for an occasional adverse comment on their system of divorce, the book uniformly bestows praise on them. As a grateful guest, Chaudhuri felt that John Bull had easily adapted himself to the loss of empire.

It was from a study of English clothes that Chaudhuri discovered there had been no foreign invasions in England. In India, the descendants of all the foreign invaders like the Aryans, the Scythians, the Huns, the Muslim, and the British have created great sartorial variety. These facts have led Chaudhuri to explain the differences in dress in philosophical terms: "Thus, we Hindus who have propounded the philosophical system of the Vedanta, which denies changes and bids us to seek salvation

only in the formless Absolute, are driven in our actions to pro-
liferate variations in the most patently biological manner, but
the Westerners who have put forward the theory of evolution
have to do everything in their power to approach the undiffer-
entiated Brahma" (p. 73). Yet, in Chaucer's Prologue to *The
Canterbury Tales*, all the pilgrims were dressed according to
their status and profession. The reason why most Europeans
dress alike now is that the economic differences are not so sharp.
Incidentally, Chaudhuri is a very keen observer of sartorial manners. He has rightly pointed out that butlers and officials put on
the same buttoned-up coat in India. As he puts it: "The buttoned-up coat had very mixed associations in British India. In
the first place, it was worn by the butlers of English homes
and clubs, and therefore nowadays when a high functionary
enters the lounge of the Gymkhana Club in New Delhi . . . it
becomes a nice point to decide whether he is a butler or a
secretary."[6]

While in England, Chaudhuri was frightened by "the eternal
silence of these infinite crowds." This was in staggering contrast
to Indian behavior where noise is an invariable concomitant of all
social intercourse. Chaudhuri has praise even for the standoffish-
ness of the English people. He says that Englishmen prefer silence
to unnecessary talk because they want to reserve their energy for
work. In contrast, Chaudhuri notes that in a bus in India, people
not only talk about their personal matters to him but also twist
his wrist to see the time from his watch even when they are
not personally known to him. He seems to bump into irresponsible
Indians most of the time. At a New Delhi bus stand, a complete
stranger once involved him in conversation about his father's
concubines, and also offered to send him mangoes. This behavior
is in sharp contrast to the reserve and taciturnity of Englishmen.

Chaudhuri praises even the negative virtues of Englishmen.
Even when an English laborer refused to talk to him in a cafe,
he did not mind it. Indeed, he was so much fascinated by the
welcome he received in England that he had to make a favorable
comment even on English cats: "At Canterbury, when I was
walking among the ruins of St. Augustine's Abbey, a cat came
up and rolled on the path before me, in order to be picked up
and tickled under the chin. When I did so it purred until I was

ready to cry, thinking of the cordial state of Indo-British friend-ship in which I had never believed" (p. 87). English cats seem to have greater expressive potential than Englishmen. Even when he found Englishmen suffering from an overdose of reticence, he treated it as a good quality. He thinks that when an English-man is friendly with someone he treats all explanations as super-fluous. Thus, Chaudhuri concludes that Englishmen never try to show off as Indians do. He fails to see that in an underdeveloped economy, until one puts all one's wares on display, one may not be noticed. If Englishmen do not talk about their personal achieve-ments, the reason is that they can afford not to do so. If Indians boast about what they have done, the reason is that they know their achievement may not otherwise be acknowledged.

While Chaudhuri has uniform praise for the Englishman's attitude toward money, his attitude toward love gets only qualified approval. Coming from a puritanical country, Chaud-huri was surprised to find that love-making was taken seriously in the West. In his opinion, India imported love from the West after tobacco and potatoes. Chaudhuri says that love-making "is Europe's special contribution to the life of passion of man-kind" (p. 118). In holding this view, he indulges in that naive antithesis, which Agehananda Bharati, the well-known author of *The Ochre Robe*, summed up succinctly in these words: "The East meditates, the West fornicates."[7] What surprised Chaudhuri was the fact that in the West the same woman who was ardently in love with her husband one year, sought relief in divorce the next. Chaudhuri's comments on this show that while he is un-orthodox in his political views, he is conservative in his attitude toward love. He believes that Western society has sacrificed many human values at the altar of love.

III *European Cultural Life*

Chaudhuri was greatly impressed by the cultural life of Europe. He was surprised to find that there was a line to buy tickets for a Shakespeare performance in Stratford-upon-Avon, and a still bigger line for a Racine performance in Paris. He found that people lived on Shakespeare and then adds, "Nobody flour-ishes on Kalidasa [in India]" (p. 141). The comparison is foolish because Kalidasa belongs to the classical Sanskrit age which is not accessible as a cultural commodity. Nobody lives on Euripides in Greece, either.

Another futile comparison made by Chaudhuri is that the Hindus care largely for politics and economics, while Englishmen care for things which he considers of greater importance. The latter are interested in art while the former concentrate on mundane things. In an unnecessary aside, Chaudhuri says: "For the great majority of my countrymen their historic civilization is a culture in the anthropologist's sense of the word. It has been reduced to its simplest to become a more or less inert psychological environment, in which they live as fish do in water" (p. 157). Civilization may not be a living reality in India, but one wonders what purpose is served by his comments. Nationalistic arguments could be made against this posture, claiming that Englishmen were savages when great civilizations flourished in ancient India, and that if the present Indian culture has come to such a sorry pass, it is to a large extent because of imperialistic exploitation.

Chaudhuri was so deeply moved by religion in England that he wanted to become a Christian (p. 176). His pro-Christian stance goes with unfavorable comparisons of Indian temples with English churches. He believes that the "Hindu pantheon is as corrupt as the Indian administration."[8] He finds that Indians worship their gods in the same way as they worship their politicians: "Between these secular prostrations and the prostrations before the gods there is only difference of degree and not of kind, because in India the most powerful political leadership is itself quasi-religious. But certainly the English people did not go to their churches to look on a Divine Ruler and his daily life" (p. 177). The answer to this anti-Indian view is that there are varieties of religious experience, and the English one is not necessarily superior. Chaudhuri thinks that the Hindu prayer is selfish and that the Hindu religion is materialistic. This is denial not only of the spirituality of India but also of the fact that religion all the world over is meant for the betterment of the human spirit. The materialism of Indian religion is perhaps partly a projection of Chaudhuri's mind.

IV   *England Today*

While in England, Chaudhuri was greatly impressed by the welfare state and surprised that, except for professional politicians, people showed little interest in politics. Compared to Englishmen, Indians are obsessed with politics. He believes that the spirit of politics is kept alive in India because the country represents a lower state of civilization. He writes: "There is also suffering and discontent enough to make it necessary for a government which calls itself parliamentary democracy to have recourse to shooting and gassing as a matter of regular administrative routine more often than any other independent country in the contemporary world" (p. 193). In order to show how well the political system in England worked, Chaudhuri denigrates India as a land of strife. He has such contempt for contemporary India that he states in a recent article in *Encounter*: "Just as the public in India hold the record for futile political demonstrations of all kinds, their Government for its part is pre-eminent among all the Governments of the present-day world for an ineffectual recourse to violence, which in every case reduces the authority of the State instead of restoring it."[9] Chaudhuri fails to analyze the English and Indian situations so that they may properly be compared and instead chooses to apply criteria for the English situation to the Indian one.

Chaudhuri forgives the British for their imperialistic acts but is angry with the Russians for holding on to their empire. He writes: "They [the Russians] and the English started their respective imperial enterprises at about the same epoch. But while the British empire has disappeared, the Russian is still going strong, and despite the gabble and din about ending European colonialism, not one man in Asia raises his voice for the liberation of the largest number of Asiatics still under White rule. The truth is that only dying empires are kicked, living ones never" (p. 194). Again, Chaudhuri applies criteria suitable for one situation to a different situation. Arguments could be made that central Asia is a more integral part of Russia than India was to England. Besides, Russian imperialism has a different economic relationship between Russia and her colonies than the outright exploitation of British imperialism. The case of Russia could also

be seen as similar to America in that just as Eastern Europe
tends to be Russian-dominated, so South American countries
tend to be American-dominated.

On the other hand, it is heartening to note that Chaudhuri did
not approve of England as far as its attitude to war is concerned.
In *The Continent of Circe*, he points out that Indians suffer
from many contradictions. In this book it is refreshing to note
that Indians are not the only people who suffer from them. He
finds the same fault in Englishmen. They also indulge in double-
talk: "They denounce the H-bomb every day and still cannot
refrain from making it. They are determined not to go to war,
and yet they allow a foreign nation (America) to have military
bases on their own soil" (p. 197). Apart from this defect, Chaudhuri was happy to see so much welfare activity in England.
There is housing, food, and clothing for every one, and the National Health Service works efficiently. Even English slums seem
satisfactory to him because they are better than the "quarters of
high civil servants of the Government of India" (p. 201). One
indirect way in which he found that England is civilized was
from "the number and prosperity of the shops dealing in antiques,
old books, and second-hand furniture" (p. 165). All in all,
Chaudhuri's days in England were a wonderful escape from the
distress which accompanies the spectacle of poverty in India.

A Passage to England contains malicious, and occasionally
pointless, comparisons with India. A large part of his book is in
fact a passage to India. Throughout the book, he argues as if
India were a defective kind of England. Such is his love for
England that he ignores the irony involved in the review of his
book, published in the London *Times*. The critics remarked: "Mr.
Chaudhuri does not appear to be seeing [England] for the first
time, but returning after years of exile." Chaudhuri quotes this
remark with apparent delight in one of his later books.[10] His
cringing attitude vis à vis the West only proves the oft-quoted
remark of Jawaharlal Nehru, "The intellectuals have failed
India."

In fact, when *A Passage to England* was released in India,
there was a lot of anger at Chaudhuri's pro-British attitude. Most
Indians thought that he had acted like Browning's "Lost Leader":

Just for a handful of silver he left us,
Just for a riband to stick to his coat—
Found the one gift of which fortune bereft us,
Lost all others she lets us devote . . .

For his expediency, Chaudhuri offered a curious explanation which shows that he prefers self-interest to national interest. In his article "Aping the West," he writes: "My book, *A Passage to England*, was not meant for reading in India, and if it has been read here too, that has been for me something earning a little foreign exchange."[11] It seems that in England, Chaudhuri was determined to please the Englishmen. Nationalistic Indians did not forgive him. Mr. Sham Lal, the distinguished editor of *The Times of India*, subtitled the review of this book "Wagging the Tail." In his next book, *The Continent of Circe*, Chaudhuri took revenge on his fellow-Indians by writing the most heretical criticism of India that he was capable of writing.

CHAPTER 4

The Hindu's European Soul

EXCEPT for the expression of an occasional nostalgia for the leisurely Hindus of ancient India, the rest of *The Continent of Circe* is written in a mood of dark despair. Chaudhuri has joined the ranks of unsympathetic commenters on India like Arthur Koestler, V. S. Naipaul and Ronald Segal. Like Naipaul's *An Area of Darkness,* defecation is the recurring theme of the book. Chaudhuri writes: "After independence, for four years, I saw people easing themselves in the park in the morning, sitting in rows. . . . Within the city I have seen streets running with sewage water and faeces floating on it, while, undisturbed by this, vendors of vegetables and other food-stuffs were selling their produce on the adjacent pavements" (p. 31). In the same vein, Naipaul writes: "Indians defecate everywhere. They defecate, mostly, beside the railroad tracks. But they also defecate on the beaches; they defecate on the hills; they defecate on the river banks; they defecate on the streets; they never look for cover."[1] It is a pity that both Chaudhuri and Naipaul are attracted to things which smell foul.

The underlying assumption of the book is that India is a defective kind of Europe. Such an oddly oriented study is bound to suffer from many faults. It is significant that while expressing his disapproval of India, Chaudhuri chooses to quote Alberuni, Babur, E. M. Forster, and Kipling. The book deals mainly with the influence of the Indian environment on Hindu character. It is full of geographical explanations and climatological philosophy. The central thesis is that the Hindus are the descendants of a European race—the Aryans—who lost their glorious heritage because of the awful climate of this subcontinent. According to Chaudhuri, the European colonists occupied India in the same way as "their collateral descendants did North America or

54

Australia at a much later age" (p. 132). The view that the Hindus
are really Europeans corrupted by the tropical environment is
Chaudhuri's eccentric original contribution to cultural anthropology. As he puts it: "The Hindu is the European distorted,
corrupted, and made degenerate by the cruel torrid environment
and by the hostility, both real and imagined, of the true sons
of the soil" (p. 131).

It is interesting to note that Chaudhuri learned about his
European origin only when he went to England: "The notion
that we Hindus were Europeans enslaved by a tropical country
became a conviction when I paid a short visit of eight weeks to
the West in 1955 at the age of fifty-seven" (p. 307). Till the age
of twenty-two, Circe cast such a spell on him that he often lived
in a state of misery. (This condition is recorded in his autobiography.) Chaudhuri slowly recovered his original soul by
forming European habits. Now he is happy: "I have rescued my
European soul from Circe, to whom it was a kind of happiness
to be in thrall" (p. 309). The purpose of this unusual view is to
show that Chaudhuri is a Hindu with a European soul. While
he has saved himself from the prevailing swinishness, other
Hindus have continued to suffer on the Continent of Circe.

I *India's Image*

It is Chaudhuri's thesis that in spite of so many foreign ob-
servers, diplomats, correspondents, and journalists, there is a
large-scale ignorance about India. The world's knowledge of
secretive India since 1947 is vitiated by contemporary requirements of international friendship and the consequent timidity.
In particular, Chaudhuri blames Indo-Anglian novelists for the
world's inaccurate knowledge of India: "The novelists, too conscious of the demand, and keen to meet it, go about the country
note-book in hand, collect local colour and turns of speech, record
snatches of conversation with special reference to such slips in
English as lend themselves to caricature, and then three quarters
in ponderous solemnity, and a quarter in cold-blooded self-
seeking malice, they turn out works which are no more fiction
than blue-books are fables" (p. 23). Here, Chaudhuri tries
to be clever rather than accurate. Nowhere has India been
depicted more imaginatively than in the Indo-Anglian novel.

For want of space, I can only give a few illustrations. A single novel of R. K. Narayanan, *The English Teacher*,[2] provides a better microcosm of Indian culture than Chaudhuri's generalizations., Mulk Raj Anand has shown a remarkable sense of social realism in his depiction of the Indian proletariat.[3] Raja Rao, in his expatriate's idealization of India, provides an interesting counterpoint to Chaudhuri's heretical portrait of his own country. G. V. Desani, in *All About H-Hatterr*, provides a much better picture of a confused Eurasian than does Chaudhuri in his autobiography. Ruth Prawer Jhabvala is more successful in depicting India's *kulturkampf* in *A Backward Place* than Chaudhuri in his article on the same subject in *Quest*.[4]

Yet Chaudhuri assumes a pose of semantic superiority over his fellow-Indians. He says that "the English words used by our political and intellectual leaders stand for very little else than the letters they are written with" (p. 37). He believes that since independence, Indians have manufactured a Nationalized Factory of Words. He himself was in thrall to words in his autobiography: he regarded England as "a Country which possessed not only beautiful spots but also place-names which sounded beautiful. Isle of Wight, Osborne House, Windsor, Grasmere, Balmoral, Holyrood Palace...."[5] Chaudhuri fails to see that the misuse of words is not a weakness of Indians alone. If a semanticist like I. A. Richards is to be believed, this symbolic distance is to be found as much in India as in the West.[6]

Chaudhuri is profoundly pessimistic about India. He advises foreigners not to work too hard in India: "Count, you Europeans take too much on your selves in our tropical country.... In India, that is not doing one's duty, but committing suicide" (p. 18). Chaudhuri claims that he has an unflinching sense of realism because, according to him, "a man who cannot endure dirt, dust, stench, noise, ugliness, disorder, heat and cold has no right to live in India" (p. 31). Dr. G. C. Pande argues against this, saying: "That India has fallen far behind the Western world in matters of public hygiene and sanitation in recent times is essentially the outcome of the grinding poverty which was the chief legacy of the British empire in India."[7] Moreover, one has only to consider the arrangements for public sanitation in the cities of the Indus Valley Civilization to realize how great Indians were when Europe was barbaric and the United States of America did not exist.

Chaudhuri's book is subtitled: "An Essay on the People of India." As far as ethnology is concerned, he classifies Indians into three groups—the Dark, the Yellow, and the Brown. This classification is derived from Herbert Risley's *The People of India*[8] from which only those details are selected which help Chaudhuri prove his points. Chaudhuri is very orthodox as far as his classification of races is concerned, but he is unorthodox in his views about the caste system. It is typical of Chaudhuri that when every one else in India speaks against the caste system, we have in him the one surviving champion of this institution. Thus he says that only a strong dose of casteism will prevent undeserving people from obtaining the high offices. "If the system suppressed anything it was only ambition unrelated to ability, and watching the mischief from this kind of ambition in India today I would say that we could do with a little more of the caste system in order to put worthless adventurers in their place" (pp. 61–62). This may entertain many readers, but it will not convince anyone.

II *The Aboriginals*

Chaudhuri's views on Indian aboriginals are as eccentric as those on the caste system. He bemoans the fact that the aboriginals are used as a cultural commodity, but no genuine affection is shown toward them. They are put on display at the annual folk dance festival arranged on the Republic Day of India, but otherwise they are treated as slaves. The Aryans show an ambivalent attitude toward these "Children of Circe" because they love their men for their primitive vigor, their women for a certain ineffable physical charm, and at the same time, they hate them for their backwardness. But Chaudhuri would like to keep them as museum pieces, because, according to him, they are the only authentic Indians. He regards them as the only true autochthons.

Chaudhuri wants the aboriginals to continue to live in their pastoral surroundings. He believes that industrialization will unnecessarily Europeanize them and put them out of tune with the Indian climate, thereby making them suffer as the Hindus do now. The only hope for the aboriginals is that "the Hindu order in its present state has neither the energy, physical and mental, nor the organizing capacity, nor perhaps the intelligence to carry through the type of industrialization which is now contemplated. ... If that happens, the isolation and the way of life of the aboriginals will not be totally destroyed, and some of them at least will escape the ruin. Circe will fight for her children and she may even now win the battle" (pp. 83–84). One cannot understand why Chaudhuri wants to keep the children of Circe innocent and the foster-children of Circe conscious of their environment.

By a curious association of ideas, Chaudhuri arrives at the conclusion that the biggest danger the aboriginals have to fear will be from the Americans. He writes: "In the fulfillment of their destiny the American people will become the greatest imperial power the world has seen, and they will repeat their history by having the blood of the Dark Indian on their head as they have that of the Red" (p. 85).

III   Indian Climate and British Behavior

Chaudhuri is sympathetic not only toward the children of Circe—the aboriginals—but also toward the victims of Circe—the British, who had to put up with the horrible climate of the subcontinent. As compensation for the climate, the British used the sturdy women of the aboriginals; they took a great interest in pornographic literature; and they became generally loose-moraled. Chaudhuri believes that Englishmen did not behave properly in India because they could not adjust to the Indian climate: "Their sense of proportion broke down, the habit of understatement disappeared, and they became extremists with an incredible stridency in their opinions, which became raw and crude."[9]

Chaudhuri could understand the causes of British behavior in India only after his trip to England. If he found a metamorphosis in his own personality during his stay of five weeks in England, this was good enough evidence for him that the British got denatured because of Circe's bad influence. The British suffered from anxiety neurosis because they could not adjust to the Indian environment. Hence they took to aggressive self-defense by believing in their infallibility. It is because of this shared de-generacy that Chaudhuri finds many common points between Hindus and the British who served in India. The latter suffered for only two hundred years, while the former have suffered for centuries. The common sins of the Commonwealth are: "race pride and sense of superiority; segregation of the conflicting elements; aggressive self-defence; suppression and unconscious ill-treatment of the indigenous population; unwillingness to share culture; and continual mental strain" (p. 130). Such sins seem somewhat extreme to have been caused by climate alone.

IV *Hindu Militarism*

One of the startling theses in *The Continent of Circe* is that Hindus are a war-mongering people. The biggest contradiction in their life is to be seen in regard to their militarism. On the one hand, they preach nonviolence, which is, moreover, only a rationalization of their cowardice; on the other hand, they are vehemently militaristic in their outlook. Ronald Segal found that even Acharya J. B. Kripalani and C. Rajagopalachari were not free from this contradiction. Mr. Segal writes: "In June 1962 . . . C. Rajagopalachari and J. B. Kripalani endorsed a call for India's unilateral disarmament. Four months later both men were flaying the Nehru Government for having failed to make adequate military preparations to meet the Chinese threat."[10]

Chaudhuri offers some varied and odd evidence to prove his point. He believes that Ashoka's inscriptions have misled us about Hindu nonviolence, and that Ashoka took to nonviolence only when there was nothing left to conquer. In fact, Ashoka could have proceeded to conquer Burma or China or Afghanistan or Iran. The thirteenth rock edict clearly shows that he desisted from further warfare because of the misery and carnage caused by the Kalinga battle. Chaudhuri ignores these facts and cites another piece of evidence from the *Mahabharata*: when Bhim kicked the dying Duryodhana, he demonstrated that the Hindus are callous. Chaudhuri does not mention the fact that Bhim's callousness is severely condemned in the *Mahabharata*. He cites the Jat guide, who blissfully told him that the Jats killed a number of Muslim women, as *proof* of blatant Hindu aggressiveness. The Maratha war cry *"Har Har Mahadeo"* is treated as an example of the Hindu's unfailing love of war. In quoting these instances from Indian history, Chaudhuri fails to see that similar conditions prevailed all over the world, including Greece and Rome, not to speak of modern Europe and the U.S.A.

Chaudhuri gave these instances from Indian history to show that the Hindus are as aggressive now as they were before. Mr. A. K. Majumdar observes: "Mr. Chaudhuri by asserting the combative nature of Hindus was preparing the ground for indicting the 'Hindu' Government of India for harbouring aggressive designs against Pakistan and against Portuguese sovereignty over Goa."[11] With sheer perversity, Chaudhuri distorts all the facts of recent history and blames India in the following terms:

Hindu militarism created the myth of military danger from Pakistan. . . . This was, however, only a vapid and negative satisfaction, and the martial Hindu soul spoiled for a fight. So the expedition to Goa was launched. . . . In regard to the conflict with China it can be asserted with confidence that it was inspired almost wholly by Hindu jingoism, with the Hindu possessiveness as a second underlying factor. (p. 107)

No arguments are presented on behalf of India, and therefore it is hard to discern the truth of the situation Chaudhuri describes. Certainly his understanding of even the events is subject to argument. Chaudhuri's version of India's war with China is strange for an Indian. He writes: "There is no doubt that the war with China has been a financial windfall for the Government, and it may be assumed that nothing short of a deep-seated and genuine militarism could have produced such readiness in the Hindus to part with money" (p. 111). He accuses even Nehru of militarism. Chaudhuri says that Nehru could not resist the temptation of letting out an operational secret when one fine morning, he announced before his departure for Ceylon, that he had asked his Generals to drive the Chinese out of NEFA (North East Frontier Agency). Even Dr. Radhakrishnan, who was President of India, is accused of misusing an academic occasion when, while congratulating Dr. P. V. Kane for his work on *Dharma Shastra*, he said that India was fighting a war of Dharma[12] against China. While a nationalist would remember China's great betrayal in supporting the slogan "Hindi-Chini-Bhai-Bhai"[13] and then attacking India, Chaudhuri blames India.

V The Hindu Paradox

Since the Hindus comprise the majority of India's population, Chaudhuri's book deals mainly with them. He rightly says that the British understood the Hindu mind only in so far as it served their interest. Certain European idealists created the myth of Indian spirituality, but they lost all these romantic notions as soon as they came in contact with the reality. They found that India is home neither of fabulous wealth nor of esoteric wisdom. Even E. M. Forster was completely disillusioned when he actually visited India. Chaudhuri points out that in *A Passage to India*, Forster "presents all the Indians in it either as perverted, clownish, or queer characters" (p. 93). Forster was satirical and uncomplimentary because the reality in India did not come up to his expectations.

E. M. Forster's contempt for Hindus provides an interesting reason for Western dislike of them. Chaudhuri feels that the Westerners applied the Renaissance norms of reason, order, and measure to Hindu behavior and found it wanting. They found that Hindu life is full of contradictions: "There was an unnatural insistence, partly realized in practice, on chastity, accompanied by a sex-obsession and sensuality in personal life whose scale and degradation had to be seen to be believed. To give another example, there was a morbid respect for animal life, going hand in hand with beastly cruelty to living creatures subject to human exploitation" (p. 94). Chaudhuri rightly points out that Westerners found the Hindu law-giver Manu's belief in metempsychosis as irrational as Lord Krishna's sexual exploits with sixteen hundred lusty young women.

This irrationality of the Hindus extends to other realms as well. Chaudhuri points out that he has seen all his life "professors of physics loaded with amulets, secularists poring over horoscopes and palms, and politicians refraining from submitting their election nominations except on auspicious days" (p. 95). These very people try to show that they are indifferent toward money and yet say that Hinduism is dying of Americanism, so that they can get promises of more money. Chaudhuri finds only paradoxes in Hindu life. Hindus fast and then overeat. They suffer from washing mania and still remain unclean. In a severe indictment, Chaudhuri points out a large number of contradictions which he has noted in the Hindu mind: "A sense of Hindu solidarity with an uncontrollable tendency towards disunity within the Hindu order; collective megalomania with self-abasement; extreme xenophobia with an abject xenolatry; authoritarianism with anarchic individualism; violence with non-violence; militarism with pacifism; possessiveness with carelessness about property owned; courage with cowardice; cleverness with stupidity" (p. 97).

In two articles entitled "Dichotomy in Hindu Life" which Chaudhuri wrote for *Quest*,[14] he provides many illustrations to support his thesis. For want of space, I can illustrate only one set of contradictions, xenophobia versus xenolatry. If Alberuni and Abbé Dubois noted xenophobia in Hindu life, this is now matched by excessive xenolatry. Not only foreign economists but even foreign scientists are much in demand in India. Chaudhuri notes with regret: "This adulation of the foreigner in the Hindu ruling order . . . is a paradox, almost a perversity. A distinguished Indian economist once told me . . . that man for man no Indian economist was inferior to any foreign economist. Yet is there any country in the world which makes use of a larger number of foreign economists?"[15] This is largely true. But while Chaudhuri has done valuable service in teaching Hindus the art of self-reliance, his other criticism of Hindus can only make them resent such a portrait of the collective Hindu personality.

VI   *Four Loyalties*

According to Chaudhuri, there are four Hindu loyalties: (1) the Vedas; (2) fair complexion; (3) the rivers; and (4) the cow. As regards the Vedas, he rights says that these are not devotional books but survive as liturgy and ritual. But he goes to great extremes when he says that the Hindus have not been able to cultivate any critical spirit because they treat the Vedas as the repository of all learning. Dr. Daya Krishna has rebutted this view: "The noting of Vedic authority, then, is a myth. It certainly cannot be the dividing line between the schools [of Indian philosophy] as has been stated by almost every text-book on the subject."[16] If the influence of the Vedas is limited even in the case of the six schools of Indian philosophy, it is much less so in Indian thought in general. Without formally repudiating the authority of the Vedas, the Indian scholars enunciated their own ideas which involved complete departures from the Vedic position. Chaudhuri ignores this scholarly tradition which has prevailed in India through the ages.

Chaudhuri believes that the Hindus love fair complexion because it has remained with them as one of the memories of the European past. The Indian climate is so bad that even the Europeans get brown in India. From this, it is easy to establish that the Hindus have slowly lost their European color over the last 3,000 years. Chaudhuri's view that the Hindus love white skin is questionable because neither Lord Krishna nor the dark beauties of the Ajanta caves have a fair complexion. In any case, Chaudhuri fails to see that the love of white skin probably is a universal phenomenon. Mr. S. Mokashi-Punekar says: "Nirad-babu does not explain to us why the Negro also has a fascination for white girls. Nor does he bother to quote Malinowski's *Sex Life of Savages* in which, on empirical evidence and with the help of photographs, Malinowski demonstrates that the Melanasian's concept of beauty is not far different from that of Europeans."[17]

The third loyalty, rivers, comes about because water is appreciated in a hot country. In a country where one has to be at the mercy of the monsoon, this appreciation is natural. The Hindus also worship their rivers because they believe that the water washes away their sins. The collective worship of two million bathers at the Kumbh Mela in Allahabad in 1962 surprises Chaudhuri, that "a collective idée fixe can produce a hyperkinesis of this order" (p. 166). He regards this river worship as irrational, and his own historical explanation is not enlightening.

The Hindus are sentimentally attached not only to rivers

but also to cows. Even when the Hindus cannot feed their cows properly, they do not try to get rid of them. Chaudhuri is of the opinion that the Hindus worship their cows because they hate the British and the Muslim habit of eating beef. His historical explanation for cow-worship is as follows: "The Ayrans had not found their humped cattle in the country, but had brought them from the Middle East and soon discovered that they would not survive in India without extra care" (p. 172). Thus the cow is as much a foreigner in India as the Hindus are.

VII *The Hindu View of Sex*

Chaudhuri's elucidation of the Hindu attitude toward sex is astute and forthright. He shows great historical sense by distinguishing between the "naturalistic" outlook and the vigor of the Vedic and Epic ages, the "romantic" refinement and delicacy of the Classical age, and the anti-Romantic phase of the later ages of decadence. But he again overemphasizes the role of climate. In his view, the Hindus wanted to seek relief from the environment, and one way was sex. In the early days, they proclaimed that "man is a creature devoted to the penis and the belly" (p. 188). With this belief, they employed many variations of the sexual object and of the sexual pose so as to obtain the maximum bliss. Chaudhuri believes that the sexual poses in Vatsyayan's *Kamasutra* are only a compensation for the vagaries of the Indian climate.

Chaudhuri points out that the Hindus did not treat sex impulse like hunger or defecation. The more they got exhausted, the more they clung to it with desperation, ignoring the calculus of pleasure. He gives examples from the *Rig Veda* where erection of the penis is adored as the highest good. Indra, the supreme warrior God, is so lecherous that he seduces the beautiful wives of the sages. Even the ancient hermitages were not without discreet adultery, for the sage Vrihaspati tried to seduce the beautiful pregnant wife of his brother, and when she refused his advances, he cursed the child with blindness. One wonders how far old myths can be taken as concrete evidence of Hindu attitudes toward sex.

It is interesting to note that Chaudhuri idealizes ancient India so far as love-making is concerned. The ancient Hindus romanticized the sexual act; and they even recommended star-gazing as an interlude during coitus. The study of Sanskrit literature shows the use of an elaborate sex symbolism. Chaudhuri says: "The Hindus succeeded in creating a *courtoisie*, as it were, of the sex act, and, if I might coin the word, also a troubadourism, with petty conceits, and gestures, and symbols. Incapable of transcending the flesh, they showed their ingenuity in etherealizing it" (p. 200). Ancient Sanskrit literature does not have the coarse priapism of Arabic literature or the prurience of *Lady Chatterley's Lover*.

In spite of Chaudhuri's familiarity with Sanskrit literature, there is one omission in his Hindu view of sex. He does not say anything about the Hindu worship of fertility cults. Dr. R. K. Kaul points out: ". . . it seems surprising to me that a scholar who is on terms of familiarity with Sanskrit literature from the *Rigveda* and the *Mahabharata* to the *Uttara-Ramacharita* of Bhavbhuti and the *Raghuvamsa* of Kalidas should fail to mention the one feature peculiar to the Hindus which has no parallel in any other religion, at least none survives till today viz. the fertility cult. True the Nandi is worshipped largely in the South but Shiva's phallus is worshipped all over the country."[18]

Chaudhuri is scathing when he describes the present phase of the decadence of Hindu society. He finds the same ambivalence in the Hindu attitude toward sex which Arthur Koestler noticed: "The Indian attitude to sex is perhaps more ambivalent and paradoxical than any other nation's. On the one hand, the rigid separation of the sexes, prudishness . . . on the other hand, the cult of the linga, a sex-charged mythology, erotic sculptures. . . ."[19] According to Chaudhuri, in Hindu sexual intercourse scratching and biting are as severe as in feline intercourse. With their violent caresses, the Hindus do not practice Gandhian nonviolence in the bed. In trying to increase pleasure in this coarse way, sensibilities declined. The woman was treated not as a human being but as an instrument for pleasure.

VIII   *Erotic Sculpture*

Erotic sculpture in India has been a source of wonder to many foreign tourists. They are perplexed to see its presence on

the walls of temples. For his part, Chaudhuri is surprised to
find that people from the West take such a keen interest in erotic
art. In a recent article, he says: "The horrified revulsion from the
erotic aspects of Hinduism has given place to admiration and the
Western interest in Hindu life has been shifted from one extreme
to its opposite."[20] In spite of this new interest, Chaudhuri does
not believe that these erotic figures represent the union of soul
and the supreme spirit. His denunciation of the erotic sculpture
on the walls of Konarak and Khajuraho is meant for foreign
consumption. One suspects that he has not said anything about
Indian music or Indian dance in the whole book because he did
not have any thing denunciatory to say about them.

Despite urging self-reliance on India, Chaudhuri continues
to invoke his foreign readers. In the manner of the harangues
of St. Paul he writes: "O foreigners who are visiting or staying in
India! I know that you go to Khajuraho and Konarak in the name
of our art and religion..." (pp. 189–90). But after telling
them that this sculpture has nothing spiritual about it, he goes
on to advise them not to "throw a veil of art on the iconography
of Hindu lust" (p. 215). Chaudhuri is just not interested in the
artistic aspect of Indian sculpture. He has perception neither for
the sublime expression nor the plasticity of form depicted in
these interlaced bodies. These figures are carved with the utmost
tenderness and sensuous beauty, but Chaudhuri sees only
pornography in them.

Chaudhuri makes a similar criticism of erotic figures on Indian
temples in *A Passage to England*. He has great admiration for
European nudes. He compares them unfavorably with the simper-
ing ladies of Konarak and Khajuraho: "Hindu art has made it
impossible to look at a nude without a leer, it has resolved flesh
to its most fleshly elements, Europeans have made it the expression of the spiritual in man."[21] Chaudhuri has a private
meaning of "spiritual" in mind, or else he would not have made
such statement. He fails to see that these erotic figures are only a
part of a complex configuration. He makes wrong comparisons
because he sees Indian erotic art out of its total context. Mr.
Richard Lannoy correctly says: "The success with which images
of explicit sexual delight serve the overall aesthetic mood of any
given temple, depends on the degree to which the artists have

brought erotic interest into harmony with other themes, such as the sacred dance and scenes from the Epics or the life of Krishna, and these, in turn, were also imbued with erotic overtones in performance."[22] Erotic figures on the walls provided a background for dancing girls, known as Devadasis, inside the temple.

Chaudhuri has no liking for this sensuous affirmation of the Hindus. He believes that erotic sculpture only gave them vicarious satisfaction. The West is wrongly interested in the *Kamasutra* and in Khajuraho, because it hopes that these substitute objects will increase their potency. Chaudhuri argues that the Hindus have a fear of impotence, hence they cannot provide what the Europeans lack. Dr. Mulk Raj Anand, in his *Kama Kala,* provides a corrective for the erratic view of Chaudhuri. Dr. Anand points out that Hindus believed in the dictum "be thyself" even as Greeks believed in the dictum "know thyself." He rightly says that "from the Vedic period onwards, the belief in the universe as the outcome of the cosmic union between the male and the female had been a fundamental aspect of the Hindu faith." The erotic figures on the temple walls only provide an objective correlative for this belief. They assert the faith in the principle "of the extension of the pleasure of the body as the vehicle of the soul in the warm, lush universe."[23]

IX *Minorities*

Chaudhuri believes that with the creation of Pakistan, Indian Muslims, who comprise nearly one-tenth of India's population, are lost between two worlds—"One dead and the other powerless to be born." There is something unnatural about their continuing to stay in India. The creation of Pakistan was the acknowledgment of two nations in India, but even this has not solved things. Chaudhuri says that Pakistan itself was created because of Hindu stupidity and cowardice. One might perhaps add that the continuance of Muslims in India shows the generosity of the majority community.

The Muslim community has not been able to integrate itself with the rest of India because it still prefers the dates of Iraq to the mangoes of India, as Chaudhuri sees it. He believes that many Indian Muslims still feel a loyalty to Pakistan. Historically,

they have earned Hindu disfavor not only because of their pan-
Islamic sympathy but also because of their earlier role in siding
with the British. Chaudhuri writes: "When they [the Muslims]
were basking in the sun of British favour, they did not remember that one day that might cancel their right to Hindu favour"
(p. 250). This hostility still persists.

So far as the present situation in India is concerned, Chaudhuri is angry not only with Indian Muslims but also with Indian
Christians. He believes that Indian Christians live in isolation,
far from the turbulence of the main currents of Indian life. He
says: "The great majority of them lead their etiolated life in
the shade, and no sun invigorates them. There is something
diffident and even pitiably dependent about them. I notice this
in any large gathering of Indian Christians" (p. 276). Chaudhuri's
dislike of Indian Christians is caused by the fact that they were
very close to the British when they were ruling India. His only
interest in them seems to lie in the fact that they have supplied
white prostitutes to the Hindus. He believes that the Indian
environment has had a degrading influence on the minority communities, and that they in turn have had a degrading influence
on the Hindus: "By making sensuality easier to satisfy and more
piquant in the satisfaction, the two communities show themselves
as the seducers of the Hindus" (p. 269). But the Hindus, in
their turn, satisfied a double passion—nationalism and sensuality
—by having a good time with white whores.

As far as the Goan Christians are concerned, Chaudhuri would
have been happy if they had remained separate from the main-
stream of Indian life. He would have been delighted if "in 1947
Goa had cut itself from India and floated away towards the
sugar islands of the south, to become a Madeira or Azores of
the Indian Ocean" (p. 267). If this had happened, then the
Goan Christians would have continued to enjoy their duty-free
vino di pasto, and combined Gregorian chants with Konkani
folk melodies. After this vision of a happy life, it is a little surprising to find that Chaudhuri compares the Indian occupation
of Goa with "Hitler's occupation of Austria" (p. 276). He is
unhappy at the merger of Goa with India because he feels
that the Continent of Circe has its degrading influence on the
gay life symbolized by the Calangute and Colva beaches.

X *Chaudhuri's Audience*

Nissim Ezekiel insightfully says about *The Continent of Circe*: ". . . the main thesis takes the form of a diabolic vision: Indians are swine."[24] If the author of this book had a little more literary talent, he would have written a satire like *Gulliver's Travels*. As it is, the destructive fury of the author makes one suspect the legitimacy of his arguments.

Despite his defective literary sensibility, Chaudhuri is determined to parade his learning. So we have quotations from Shakespeare, Milton, Pope, Coleridge, and Kipling only superficially relevant in their context.[25] Both irrelevance and lack of sensitivity can be seen in the case of his faulty view of D. H. Lawrence. He says:

The trouble with D. H. Lawrence was that he was a literary genius from the most vapid and insignificant class of human beings which has so far evolved in history, namely, the modern urban lower middle-class of the West. Next, intuition and not intellect being his forte, he could never perceive when he was being driven by his genius and when by his itch to rebel in a very lower middle-class manner. Besides, men from this class have a natural grievance against women of rank. . . . They satisfy a double passion: lust and class-hatred. (p. 202)

In so far as this view applies to *Lady Chatterley's Lover*, it may be feasible, but as a generalization about Lawrence, it is superficial. The shallowness of Chaudhuri's views can be seen from the fact that he does not approve of the current Western interest in the classic manuals of eroticism written in India. His argument against Vatsyayana's *Kamasutra* is that it applies "cerebration to a field where cerebration is not applicable" (p. 216). To praise Lawrence for his intuition and to denigrate Vatsyayana for his cerebration only shows that Chaudhuri can have his cake and eat it too.

Chaudhuri's contempt for Hindu erotica runs side by side with his general contempt for Hindu philosophy and Hindu thought. He feels that Western writers have unnecessarily intellectualized Indian philosophy: "Much of the modern writing on the subject is just dry as dust, choking, and soul-stripped logic-chopping, which belabours the mind until it feels sick of Hindu philosophy" (p. 147). His criticism of Hindu philosophy is as superficial as that of Benjamin Walker who dismissed it as an "arid metaphysical region."[26] It is Chaudhuri's presupposition that the Hindus can never be right, hence he reserves his worst sneers for Hindu thought: "There is no such thing as thinking properly so called among the Hindus, for it is a faculty of the mind developed only in Greece, and exercised only by the heirs of the Greeks. A very large part of what is called Hindu thinking is woolly speculation or just mush" (p. 151). Since Chaudhuri knows little Sanskrit and the mainsprings of Hindu thought are not available to him, he really has no right to make this sweeping statement. His cavalier attitude toward indology only shows that though the British Empire has disappeared from India, its ghost still survives in Chaudhuri.

This can also be seen from Chaudhuri's hatred of Hindu asceticism. He believes that the Hindus deliberately inflicted pain on themselves so that they could neutralize the pain of the environment. His statement that the Hindus love power is a crude exercise in Adlerian psychology. Through self-torture, the Hindus only wanted to assert their superiority over others: "The Hindus have always worshipped power for power's sake, and there is nothing they yearn for more than the removal of external checks on their desires and aspirations" (p. 184). Yet the motive for power is inbred in every human being. Does not Chaudhuri himself want to wield power by exposing his countrymen before the Westerners? Mr. Dilip Chitre pertinently remarks: "It appears that an acute sense of insecurity in his own society, a craving for status and acceptance, and a desire to identify himself with the ruling elite culturally and emotionally, have all been decisive factors in Mr. Chaudhuri's formulations of his views."[27]

The only operative level at which Chaudhuri's *The Continent of Circe* works is as propaganda for the Hindu middle class. He says of the foreign experts in India that, "the two things in India they ignore most and even dismiss as unimportant are Hinduism and agriculture" (p. 30). He himself can be easily accused of ignoring at least one of them. Rural India, the non-middle-class India, is inaccessible to him and he is blissfully unaware of agriculture. The villager does not bother to seek a triumph over Chaudhuri's "Circe," nor does he worry whether he is missing something in life. Chaudhuri forgets that the way to conquer the environment is not by defying it but by learning to live with it as many contented Indians have done.

Chaudhuri does not like brown colonialism in present-day India. Instead, he believes that Indians can have an industrial revolution "fully, naturally, and freely, by recovering our original European spirit and character, and conquering so far as we can the Indian environment" (p. 307). With this aim, he wants all Western mercenaries thrown out of India and the Hindus to proudly declare: "We are Europeans in our own right, and we want no patronage. We shall take destiny in our hands, create our life, and renovate our economy through our own strength, mental and physical" (p. 308). Janus indeed has two faces.

CHAPTER 5

To Live or Not to Live

CHAUDHURI'S first three books were written explicitly for a Western audience and brought him wide recognition in the West. This success has given him a position of authority as an outstanding social and political commentator on India, and he has used his prestige to bring about some valuable changes in Hindu society. His collection of articles, *To Live or Not to Live*, is subtitled "An Essay on Living Happily with Others." A shrewd analysis of family and social life, it is intended to enable other Indians to achieve happiness, since "we Indians as a people possess a remarkable genius for being unhappy ourselves and making others unhappy" (p. 195). Chaudhuri sets out to trace the causes of unhappiness and thereby help others avoid misery in India. The following passage is characteristic: "That [happiness] comes from realizing some great purpose or working for it to the best of one's ability. After that it comes from performing one's duties in life without flinching. . . . A man who is not happy with fellowmen and members of his family may find a compensating happiness in his vocation or in his duty, but he will never be fully happy" (p. 196). These lines show that Chaudhuri has outgrown the anger expressed in *The Continent of Circe*. The new mellow tone of his writing shows his desire to make a truce.

To Live or Not to Live presents a wide variety of topics. Chaudhuri discusses urban conditions in India; the forms and occasions as well as the spirit and content of social life; marriage; the extended family and the nuclear family in India; working and non-workng women; post-independence Indian youth; the relations between the sexes; and Indian attitudes to work, money, status, religion, food, etc. There the brilliant journalist reveals his talent. He has compiled a book of the articles which evoked the greatest controversy in Indian newspapers. The general intro-

72

duction and concluding summary shape this into a real book instead of a mere compilation of articles; and the prologue and the epilogue add dimension by revealing Chaudhuri's guiding principles. In spite of his usual fervor, Chaudhuri is simple, direct, and persuasive.

By his persistent preoccupation with fundamental values and basic attitudes, Chaudhuri provides a brilliant criticism of Hindu society. He is sharply observant, lively and thoughtful and has raised many Indians' consciousness. For example, he complains that most Indians do not live; they merely exist. Some aspire for money, while others care only for their survival but no one really lives. As he puts it: "I can get only two versions of living. Those who have done well in the worldly sense say that they have so much money or property; and those who have not, say that they contrived to remain alive. One group mistakes acquisition for living, and the other surviving for living. Beyond that their conception of life does not reach out. Most people sacrifice living for livelihood, a minority which consider themselves lucky for affluence. None live" (p. 8). In such a passage, Chaudhuri is radical and hard-hitting. He wishes to shake Hindu society out of its old lethargy.

This book makes one realize that Indian society is a Procrustean bed. Chaudhuri hates conformity in social life. He strongly believes that genius is essentially abnormal. About himself, Chaudhuri says: "I take it as the highest recognition of my efficacy as a writer that the fossils in the bureaucracy and academic life call me eccentric" (p. 9). Chaudhuri values his own eccentricity because he has lived for an ideal in his life. Like a character in Robert Frost, he has combined his "vocation with his avocation." Hence, Chaudhuri regards himself as an unusul Hindu and bemoans the lack of idealism in his fellow-Hindus. Even young men, intellectuals, and armchair leftists, aspire only to affluence. For this reason, there is no sense of living with dedication and purpose.

I *Calcutta and Delhi*

If Chaudhuri's autobiography was remarkable for its portrait of Calcutta, this book provides brilliant description of the social life in the capital of India. In his first book, Chaudhuri points out that after reading McDougall's *Social Psychology*, he found out the difference between sociability and gregariousness. He forthrightly says that the Bengalis of Calcutta possess gregariousness without sociability: "No better connoisseur of company was to be found anywhere in the world, and no one else was more dependent on the contiguity of his fellows, with the same incomprehension of his obligation towards them. The man of Calcutta found the company he needed so badly and continuously readily assembled, without any effort on his part, in his office, or in his bar-library, or in his college, which were no less places for endless idle gossip than for work."[1]

In Calcutta, Chaudhuri found utter boredom side by side with an unusual love of money. He says in a critical vein: "... if an Indian's love of money or his conviction of the sanctity of self-interest converts all his conversation into shop-talk, it is his gregarious propensity which makes the shop-talk so interminable. What is applicable to Indian society as a whole, I found eqully or more applicable to the Bengali society of Calcutta."[2] Chaudhuri's description of life in Calcutta is interesting because it is supported by evidence to which he alone has drawn such pointed attention.

His portrait of Delhi also shows that his impressions and opinions constitute his whole life, the stuff of his daily round, at work and in relaxation. While social life is lacking in Calcutta, in Delhi people know only how to eat well and dress well, so that he reaches the point of avoiding people to avoid their inane conversation. Chaudhuri complains that yet even at home, the Punjabis come to collect their money at odd hours in the afternoon and disturb his siesta. It is on this account that big cities like Delhi or Calcutta are "unfavourable to kindly human relations, or any human relations at all" (p. 19). Chaudhuri does not have a sense of belonging to Delhi, though as a writer he has wide contacts.

According to Chaudhuri's conception of social life, some exists in Delhi in the relations between the foreign, and more especially the Western, residents of Delhi and their Indian friends and acquaintances. He finds great sincerity and pleasantness in European social life, although apparently some Indians misuse this social life for their own selfish ends. He cites the example of an Indian who phones a foreigner and offers to attend a party to which he has not received an invitation. This is an extreme case but hardly an isolated one.

It is Chaudhuri's contention, in fact, that only foreigners possess social life in India, as may be seen from the following passage: "Thus I can also say that, although my knowledge of ancient India is not derived from a foreign medium of knowledge like the English language, my knowledge of the ruling order in modern India is entirely the product of my social relations with foreigners, or, in other words, gained through a foreign social medium" (p. 36). It is unfortunate that those Indians who have any cultural interests depend on outsiders for the satisfaction of their mental life and that even the intellectual life in India is provided by intelligent foreigners. What is true of Delhi applies to the whole of India: social life comprises mostly futile chatter.

II *Some Social Occasions Examined*

One of the social occasions in India which arouses the most interest is the wedding. There is so much interest in marriage that certain wealthy and idle men spend a lot of money on the wedding of their dolls and kittens. At more normal weddings, elaborate cooking preparations are made for the whole day. Chaudhuri is not overstating when he says: "The wedding procession appears to be more a military expedition undertaken as a punitive raid on an enemy stronghold than a friendly affair" (p. 43). It is reflection on Indian society that Chaudhuri has to use a martial metaphor to describe an Indian marriage. The long procession of the bridegroom's party gives the impression that the members are going to conquer the bride literally. The accompaniment of noise at wedding feasts makes any true socializing impossible.

Another occasion of Indian social life is the death ceremony. As at the marriage ceremony, so here, some guests arrive who never knew the person who has died. Chaudhuri rightly says: "At all events, I find no trace in these visitors of any awareness of the awful fact that death is the perpetual companion of life. They seem to consider that it is a contingent risk not to be taken seriously" (p. 47). The *sradh* ceremony which follows the death

of a person is for anybody who wants to come and eat and has
therefore become "a means of advertising one's wealth and
position" (p. 46).

The third occasion which makes Indian social life look so
unpleasant is the serious illness of a person. Even when the
patient needs rest and isolation, people come and gossip merrily.
In his characteristic way, Chaudhuri says: "It is the traditional
Indian habit of making illness, and more especially a serious
illness, as frivolous a social gathering as a cocktail party in
New Delhi" (p. 50).

Chaudhuri's dissatisfaction with Indian social life arises from
the fact that his norms are borrowed from Western social life.
Mr. Nissim Ezekiel perceptively points out: "Mr. Chaudhuri in
his rage is not expressing a surface exasperation but a profound
concern and involvement. His point of view has deep roots in a
positive philosophy which is derived from the Western intellectual, cultural, social and artistic tradition."[3] This assessment
is acute because the main reason why there is no social life in
India is the fact that there is no interest in the individual personality. Chaudhuri characteristically says: "It is a regimented
society in which the individual is only a pawn. In this society
every individual has to be dull, and thus cease to be individual,
in order to enable the collective entity called Hindu society
to survive, and to do so as a fossilized community" (p. 58).
Economic hardships have further made social life difficult.

As a sensitive individual, Chaudhuri finds many defects in
Indian social life. Most Indian families treat a social party as an
occasion where they can show off their affluence. The party to say
goodbye to a well-known figure going abroad at which the chief
guest arrives late with his family and leaves after eating, while
the other guests are asked to wait, exemplifies one of the innumerable forms of discourtesy and degradation which are common in Indian social life. The worst thing at these parties is the
malicious gossip about those who are absent. Good conversation presupposes the cultivation of the mind, and Indian
life just does not provide the required solitude so that these
traits can be developed. Instead, there is too much idle gossip
so that there is no energy left to discuss "China and Kant"
intelligently.

The main reason for the lack of social life in India, however, is sex segregation. Thus, in a gathering, one is not allowed to look at the faces of women so that one can only guess their personalities. In his autobiography, Chaudhuri narrates how villagers used to react naively to women. They used to guess the identity of women by saying "Look that slim one in the red sari is the wife of so and so," and again pointing to another, "that plump one in the green is the wife of so and so."[4] In four articles entitled "Why I Hate Indians," Chaudhuri brilliantly sums up the Indian attitude to sex as "the refuse heap of the sexual obsessions and inhibitions."[5] He points out that the Hindus cannot think that men and women can meet for purposes other than sex. But in the interests of social life, Chaudhuri is willing to permit some adultery so that the Hindus can have a full life. To make a modest beginning, he has started "the Baroque habit of kissing the hands of countrywomen" (p. 81). He is of the opinion that Indian women can revitalize social life in India.

III   *The Extended Family*

Chaudhuri gives greater importance to family life than to social life for the attainment of happiness. He defines family life as "the life of a human unit consisting of a man, his wife, and his minor sons" (p. 91). In this way, Chaudhuri's views about family life are as much derived from the European example as his ideas about social life. It is not surprising to find that Chaudhuri has no liking for the extended family. Even in his first book, he expressed his dissatisfaction with the whole system. He noted that the older people in the extended family were the most selfish. They needed the least but had the most opulent part of the meal. Their selfishness was matched only by the spoiled children, who, even in illness, were given sweets secretly by their doting mothers. The worst feature of these families was the malice that one woman could bear for another. While they were busy quarreling, the children were looked after by old servants about whom Chaudhuri writes: "Loyalty was the forte of these servants and love of power the foible."[6]

Historically, the extended family in India has been associated with early marriage and economic security. Chaudhuri finds its origin in the tribal "cooperative society based on the blood-tie" and ascribes its continuance to the "love of power of the patriarchs and the desire in the members of the family for economic security" (p. 97). At present, the extended family has many variations in India like having common property, or having separate cooking but living in one house. Though the system is crumbling in various ways, its evils have persisted. Absence of individuality and lack of initiative are two outstanding evils of the system. Thus, if the married sons get salaried jobs in the same place, they invariably live with their father under one roof even when they can afford to live separately. That is why Chaudhuri writes: "Even when a unitary family exists in fact and *ad hoc,* the emotional and theoretical attachment to the joint family survives in spite of the forced separation of the sons from their parents" (p. 104).

Chaudhuri is very critical of the patriarchal aspect of the extended family. The father has been so much a symbol of authority in the extended family that, while talking, the son is not supposed to look into his face. The result is that no son develops his own personality. There is no spirit of adventure or self-help because all sons inherit property. Besides, the persistent chatter of women makes any individual achievement difficult. The worst defect of the extended family is that the husband and wife cannot be intimate with one another. They remain inhibited throughout the day because of the presence of others. At least, the elderly married couples have the freedom to talk about money, but the young couple have only to wait for the night. Even the children are looked after by the grandmother.

According to Chaudhuri, another evil which results from the extended family can be seen in the recurrent quarrels between the mother-in-law and the daughter-in-law. The mother-in-law who cries out to the daughter-in-law at the slightest provocation, "What sort of woman is your mother who did not teach you this?" is one of several millions whose contribution to human misery in India is incalculable. It is for this reason that in his very first book, Chaudhuri regarded the mother-in-law and daughter-in-law relationship as "the fundamental aberration of Indian life."[7] Chaudhuri's mother was so bitterly cursed by her mother-in-law that she did not recover from the harmful effects for the whole of

her life. In most extended families, the poor son is caught between
two loyalties because he does not know whether he should support his mother or his wife. From all the above-mentioned points
of view, Chaudhuri arrives at the conclusion that the extended
family has outlived its utility. He makes a strong plea to end
it: "What is called for is an abandonment of the whole idea of
the joint family, large or small, in principle and in practice. If
family life is to be established on a proper basis in India this
must be done" (p. 132).

IV   *The Working Woman*

The new phenomenon in India, which Chaudhuri thoroughly
disapproves of, is the arrival of the working woman who
waits for marriage but is not able to marry. While one
can understand his enthusiasm for the disappearance of the
extended family, it is difficult to account for his dislike of working women. He says: "I regard the emergence of the working
women, unmarried as well as married, as the greatest threat to
the family in every country and society, and as even a greater
threat in India and Indian society" (p. 133). He regards the
working women as symbols of decadence and cheap imitation
of the West. And he gives the examples of aristocratic women
who did not work and made substantial contribution to culture.

Chaudhuri is very orthodox as far as his attitude to working
women is concerned. He argues that even when a working
woman is able to marry, she harms the children. But Indian
society is so wretched that even working women are not able
to marry. Marriage for love is not possible in a society where
there is sex segregation. Chaudhuri writes: "Unfortunately, Hindu
society will neither organize 'love marriage" nor reorganize arranged marriage" (p. 138). As things are in India, at present, there
is a great loss of values. For the poor working girl, there is hope
of marriage in the beginning but subsequently only disillusionment.

Chaudhuri is not a sound student of economics. He claims
that, in this age of economics, he is contemptuous of the whole
subject. It is out of this ignorance that he makes the following
statement: "I strongly maintain that if family life is to be saved

as something of irreplacable value, the income of one member of a family should be adequate to maintain the whole family on a civilized standard of living" (p. 148). His argument against the working woman is that jobs are limited in India; hence men should work, while the women should look after the home. If leisure is essential for the development of personality, so is money. The argument that jobs are limited in India does not hold because certain jobs are done better by women. Chaudhuri does not want living equated with livelihood, yet for most middle-class families in India, livelihood itself is a problem. While he expects men to do more work and earn more money, one wonders why he expects women to be sexual drudges at home? His own example does not help because neither are all men as gifted as he is nor are all women as devoted as his wife is.

It is difficult to understand why Chaudhuri does not want the Westernization of Hindu society as far as working women are concerned. He believes that the happiness of the family can be increased if the women look after the home. One fails to understand why this happiness cannot be increased if the woman adds to the family income and leads a busy life. In any case, the empirical evidence disproves Chaudhuri. If a sociologist like Promilla Kapur is to be believed, working women have enabled many families to lead a fuller and richer life. Mrs. Kapur writes: "The status of working women in India has no doubt changed and is changing. It has improved a lot from the stage when it was considered derogatory for a middle- or upper-class woman to come out of the four walls of her home to take up gainful employment."[8] Chaudhuri, however, continues to be orthodox in his attitude to working women.

V Marriage in Hindu Society

Chaudhuri regards fruitful married life as an essential requirement of a good society. But Hindu society has not given love its due. In Western society, one loves and then marries; in Hindu society, one marries and then loves. As it is, in present-day India, people marry neither in Indian nor in Western style. This has led to a great confusion of values. Chaudhuri, who himself married at the age of thirty-four in the orthodox Hindu style, saw his bride only when he was about to enter the marital bed. It is interesting to note that the same man, in his maturity, now pleads for the modernization of Hindu society.

Chaudhuri believes in the geometry of love, which is primarily visual. He writes: "Without seeing there is no loving, and no man can love a woman if the geometrical properties of her body do not tally with his geometrical predispositions, which will control his aesthetic and amorous inclinations" (p. 156). The young man, who married without seeing his wife, now says: "How to train the choice in ellipses is therefore the question" (p. 157). Each person is born with inborn likes and dislikes. Chaudhuri wants everyone to satisfy the inclinations of his mind.

Instead of allowing everyone to seek the waistline of his choice, Hindu society has reduced marriage to a market transaction. Marriage in India is not a human proposition. Matrimonial advertisements in newspapers are a clear evidence of Hindu degradation. Chaudhuri gives a pathetic instance of a Vaidya Bengali girl who is a permanent lecturer in a Delhi college and proficient in French. Even she has to be married off by an advertisement in the paper—"convent education, 23 years old, tall (164 cm), slim, fair." But she is not an isolated instance. Many other Indian girls of her age are in the same plight because marriage has become a matter of money and status only.

Chaudhuri's dissatisfaction with the Indian system of marriage was expressed in his very first work. He describes Indian marriages there in these terms: "Marriages may be personal events in the West, with us they are family events, and if anybody denies that there can be drama and romance in such marriages he should come and see for himself what the demoniac energy and meddlesomeness of third parties can make of the union of passive firsts and seconds."[9] The tone of this sentence clearly shows that he is writing a sociological tourist guide for the occidental.

But in his second work, Chaudhuri surprised everyone by denouncing the Western system of marriage as frivolous. He does not like the Western system of divorce. It is surprising that in *A Passage to England*, the Hindu system of marriage got unqualified approval and uniform praise. Thus, Chaudhuri wrote:

"We are often told by our Western friends that they just cannot understand our system of marriage. Most of us do not understand theirs either. In any case, countless millions have found happiness in our system, and it is not to be spoken of lightly."[10] This is a flattering compliment, but the Hindu system of marriage, at present, is not as successful as Chaudhuri makes it out to be. Hindu culture offers no alternative to unsuccessful marriage. A poor husband has to put up with a nagging wife, or a devoted wife has to put up with a vicious husband. Since Hindu society makes marriage a life-long permanent contract, there are so many unhappy marriages which just continue because of sacramental sanctity.

The institution of marriage has been fast deteriorating in India because of the faulty system of arranged marriage. The parents have ceased to be a cultural influence on their children. Hence it is difficult to determine the cultural status of a family. It is for this reason that the earlier guarantee of family reputation is missing in Hindu society. Chaudhuri writes: "Most arranged marriages today are very speculative business transactions, in respect of personal relations even when not in respect of money" (p. 168). The worst aspect of arranged marriages is that they do not treat love as the basis of marriage. They prove to be a gamble because, in most cases, they stifle the natural affections of the soul. Chaudhuri wisely says: ". . . the unnatural segregation is the most cruel and frustrating thing in contemporary Hindu society. This starvation of natural cravings results either in a deadening of the sensibilities, or in continuous suffering, or in a wild and perverted breaking out" (p. 171). This unnatural segregation of the sexes is the main reason for the frustration of Indian youth. In such conditions, it is only natural that Indian society is oriented toward acquisition rather than achievement.

To Live or Not to Live makes some valuable suggestions for some fundamental changes in Indian society. If young men and women are allowed to meet before a formal proposal for marriage is made, many unhappy marriages could be avoided in India. Chaudhuri makes a sound proposal that young men and women in India should know about one another before they can decide the issue that will affect the whole of their lives. This is a useful suggestion which shows Chaudhuri's concern for

the reformation of Hindu society. But it is suprising that he
wants the Westernization of Hindu society as far as marriage
is concerned, while he is conservative in his views about the
working woman.

VI   *The Nuclear Family*

Chaudhuri is so Westernized that he regards the nuclear
family as the ideal type of family. It is only in this sort of
family that one imbibes the culture of parents. There is some
impersonal tone in each good family which passes from generation to generation. But there is so much dullness in Hindu life
that a good life is just not possible. Chaudhuri writes: "I have
observed that in most cases the observed lack of vitality in India
is brought by self-indulgence, that is, surrender to propensities
which eat into both physical and mental powers" (pp. 177-78).

The worst thing in the Hindu extended family is that children
are not allowed to develop their personalities. Chaudhuri's
nuclear family provides an exception to this rule. As a fond
father and devoted husband, he not only has inculcated the
reading habit into his sons but also has initiated them into Western music. But in most other Hindu families the members suffer
from conflict of interests or they have no interests at all. This
absence of taste causes the decline of culture.

Chaudhuri's norms of a good family are all borrowed from
the West. All his examples of an ideal family are taken from
Germany or England. Hence he is very critical of those Hindu
families which suffer from conflict of interests. He prefers divorce
to unnecessary bickering. But Chaudhuri is a confused mixture
of the East and the West. He does not like the Western idea of
divorce, yet he partly believes in Hindu partriarchalism.

Chaudhuri bemoans the fact that there is no proper division
of labor in a Hindu family. Some Hindu women show their
peversity by ignoring the house. They consider it below their
dignity to look after domestic work. Chaudhuri comments "Nearly
all women take the view that any kind of responsibility for the
proper management of the home is the exploitation of the woman
by the man" (p. 187). Since even non-working women do not
share the burden of the family, this inequality of labor leads to

frequent conflicts. This tension becomes more conspicuous when the wife is dominating.

The conflict of generations is another cause of unhappiness in the Hindu family. Most Hindu parents are unusually selfish toward their children. Hence the young ones are not able to develop their personality fully. Chaudhuri writes: "Most parents are sordidly materialistic and worldly, and do not show any appreciation of the intangible values of life" (p. 193). It is the absence of this type of idealism which has ruined family life in India. Most fathers are so busy with the problem of living that they do not live at all. Chaudhuri gives significant instances from certain distinguished German families so that the Hindus can emulate their example.

VII *Hindu Society at the Crossroads*

In a recent article entitled "Our Unsocial Social Life," Chaudhuri points out what he considers the various defects of Hindu society to be. He writes: "Hindu society is basically genetic in its outlook, and looks upon social life only as an extension of the family, clan or tribe. It is very difficult for us to get out of this mould of social life, which is really tribalism and to acquire genuinely social behaviour."[11]

To Live or Not to Live presents other evils which are conspicuous in present-day Hindu society. Characteristically, Chaudhuri generalizes on the basis of his personal experiences. The young man who told him, "I don't care about idealism or faith. I shall be satisfied with a good job," speaks for millions of educated Indians. A ten-year-old boy is impressed by a three-year-old cousin because he is very rich, which shows that corruption has seeped down to the youngest of the young. The pretty young secretary who worked in Chaudhuri's office and was pursued by the entire male staff symbolizes the plight of the working woman in India. No other Indo-Anglian writer has portrayed the ills of Indian society as well as Chaudhuri has here.

CHAPTER 6

Between Tradition and Modernity

*T*he Intellectual in India is the first in a series "Tracts for the Times" in which leading scholars discuss the crucial problems that face India today. Mr. C. Paul Verghese rightly says: "The general title owes its inspiration to the famous tracts of the Oxford movement in England in which many leading figures took part in a fight against the challenge of materialism posed by the Industrial Revolution. The series in India too is likewise intended to combat the evils from which India is suffering today."[1]

In Chaudhuri's preface to the book he writes:

All over India those who have any intellectual ambitions and aptitudes are discouraged. Authoritarianism in politics and social life which runs deep among the Hindus, hostility or apathy to intellectual activities, the precarious economic situation of the intellectual who has most often to sell himself to make a livelihood—have all tended to make him feel frustrated if not wholly paralysed. I want to tell him that the situation is not as bad as he imagines, and it is largely a question of his own faith, energy and intelligence. I have in every case suggested practical means of overcoming his difficulties.

Chaudhuri's book is therefore to be a manual for the intellectual in India.

This work may be interestingly compared with one written on the same subject by Edward Shils, a noted American sociologist. Whereas Chaudhuri's work is historical in its intention, that of Shils is sociological. Chaudhuri presents the etiology of the disease and its diagnosis and then suggests how the Indian intellectual can best recover from the malady. Shils' concerns are more immediate. He sees the problems of the Indian intellectual in relation to contemporary Indian society and arrives

85

at the following conclusion: "The problems of the Indian intellectual will find their solution, to the extent that any problems are solved, in the emergence of traditions and institutions which foster individuality and creativity. If the Indian intellectual can come into a situation in which he perceives and accepts real tasks, then he will draw on whatever resources are within himself and his cultures, traditional and modern, to solve them."[2] Shils' analysis is surprisingly shrewd and penetrating considering the short time he spent in India.

Compared with Shils' work Chaudhuri's superficial analysis only shows that Indian intellectuals lack depth. In writing this book, he has ignored his own dictum which he set forth in his brilliant article on Indian intellectuals: "No original and powerful thinking can come except from long immersion in a set of concrete facts, which, so to say, ignite themselves to produce real thought."[3] In fact, Chaudhuri's study lacks the broad sweep and concrete evidence which Shils found missing generally in Indian intellectuals. Shils noted with regret that among Indian intellectuals, there is "a lack of ferment, a deficient vigor, an impoverishment of curiosity, a feebleness of the forward reach."[4] Chaudhuri's book only provides an illustration of Shils' indictment.

Chaudhuri seems to have two standards—one for the British and the other for his Indian publishers. When he writes for the former, he tends to be exacting and meticulous, but for the latter, he tends to be careless and slipshod. This book lacks the finish and polish of his earlier work and could be criticized by applying his criticism of other Indian intellectuals to his own case: "Intellectual work in India lacks both solidity and volume, and the output is thin as well as superficial. . . . An intellectual becomes more shoddy as he becomes more and more mature in age."[5] It is a pity that Chaudhuri's own case only illustrates the pitfalls of other Indian intellectuals.

I Three Traditions

Chaudhuri recognizes three distinct intellectual traditions—the Hindu, the Muslim, and the modern—which existed at the beginning of the present century. The Hindu tradition was concerned "with the maintenance of Dharma, i.e., the general Hindu way of life with a religious sanction behind it" (p. 1). In this tradition, Sanskrit was studied as the main source of Hindu thought. Brahmins were highly placed in society and were given special gifts by their disciples. The student lived with his *guru*,[6] who, with his specialized knowledge of philology, lexicography, and etymology, provided exegesis of texts. In such an atmosphere, there was intellectual wrestling: "The established scholars had jousts among themselves, and the ambitious young ones challenged their own position and reputation by overthrowing them" (p. 4). Even Western Indologists depended on these Pundits for the authoritative interpretations of texts. The two outstanding scholars in this tradition were Ishwar Chandra Vidyasagar and Swami Dayanand Saraswati.

The Islamic tradition had the same faith in the exegesis of texts. The correct interpretation of Islamic sacred law was treated as the highest intellectual effort. Chaudhuri points out that the hallmark of the Muslim tradition was "the continuation of the divinely ordained Islamic way of life, and . . . a correct interpretation of the *Shariiah,* or Islamic sacred law" (p. 5). In this Muslim tradition, the learned man or *Ulema* was even more influential than the Pundit in the Hindu tradition. It was this feeling of the separateness of Muslim intellectual tradition that gave rise to the theocratic state of Pakistan. Chaudhuri mentions Sir Syed Ahmed Khan, Mohammed Ali Jinnah and Iqbal as the most distinguished intellectuals who belonged to this tradition.

The third intellectual tradition in India had its beginnings among those who received Western education. This was welcomed by the new elite in India because it created the modern life based on the Western pattern. As Chaudhuri puts it: "It was an instance of cultural colonialism, but a colonialism welcomed by the people, who belonged to the dispossessed native cultural system" (p. 9). This gave rise to the intellectual in the Western sense and the wide cleavage between Hindu and Western tradition. It is interesting to note that all three traditions converged in Raja Rammohan Roy who was the pioneer of the Indian Renaissance. As a result of his effort, prose appeared in its new form for the first time in modern Indian languages. Not only in literature, but in politics, religion, and social reform, the Westernized intellectuals wielded greater influence than those belonging to the other two traditions. Their mastery of the English language and their familiarity with European rationalism gave them a position of authority in India so long as India was under British rule.

II *The Revival of Learning*

It was as a result of the Western influence that the Indian Renaissance started in the nineteenth century. According to Chaudhuri, the nineteenth-century Hindu intellectuals were led to undertake four major inquiries which were: "(1) What were the shortcomings of their own institutions and outlooks, and how were they to be removed? (2) How was national self-respect and confidence to be revived? (3) In what manner were the in-coming and irresistible elements of Western culture to be absorbed and combined with their own traditions? (4) What attitude was to be adopted towards British rule and, since in the ultimate analysis the only aim could be political independence, how was it to be secured?" (p. 15). These are the fundamental enquiries which gave rise to the Indian Renaissance. At this time, it was generally believed that subjugation was the chief cause of intellectual decline and that suffering in India was caused by lack of enlightenment. Hence all Indian thinkers laid emphasis on the psychological approach to political questions.

It was this contact with the West that taught the Hindus to think historically and to study their past scientifically. The re-discovery of ancient Indian philosophy gave rise to the belief that Hindus are materially backward but morally superior, so that Chaudhuri says: "Thus modern Hindus, too, when they acquired historical consciousness, came to regard themselves as a chosen people, who might be politically and militarily weak but had a right to teach spiritual values and morality to the rest of the world" (p. 25). It was also believed that since India provided the ground for the fusion of Aryan and Dravidian cultures, India could be the place where the East and the West could meet in the best possible way.

Chaudhuri's views on the Indian Renaissance are hackneyed

reformulations of ideas which he had already expressed more tellingly in his autobiography. In both the books, Chaudhuri makes the same observation that Indian thought is derivative and imitative. Even when Indians developed the Western modes of thought, they depended on Western intellectuals to supply them with social, political, and economic ideas:

The modern intellectual effort of Indians always had a large amount of pure imitation in it, for it was trying to transplant the forms and results of Western thought to this country. . . . In the past Indian thought in its creative aspect always tried to bring about an adaptaion of the ideas of the West in order to apply them to wholly different psychological and material conditions. As a result, their thinking was not the kind of thinking by rote that Indian thought has become now. It was a positive, selective and assimilative thinking, which brought the thought in close relation with the realities in India. (p. 40)

III *Religion, Materialism, and the Intellectual*

Chaudhuri arrives at the pessimistic conclusion that intellectual activities have less effect on Indian society as a whole than should be expected. He points out: "For the vast masses of Indian peasants and artisans, constituting more than nine-tenths of the population, the intellectual activities meant nothing at all." (p. 27). Only the exceptionally small proportion of Indian Society that is middle-class is amenable to intellectual ideas, but these few have made no impact on the masses. As Chaudhuri puts it: "The part of the middle-class which counted for any serious consideration of the influence of intellectual activity was constituted entirely by men belonging to the liberal professions and the higher ranks of the civil service" (p. 29). Even in this class, women did not take any part in intellectual life and therefore had no effect on the minds of children.

Because of the prevailing anti-intellectual atmosphere, even full-time intellectuals could not find support from the environment. Chaudhuri notes with regret that "intellectual life in India is something like a broadcasting system which has only transmitters but no receivers."[7] In a greater proportion of families than in the West, intellect was used to gain worldly goods, or at best, it was a symbol of social status. There were very few peo-

ple who pursued the intellectual life for its own sake. The
peculiarly Indian factors of superstition and magic were at the
root of the problem. According to Chaudhuri: "The numbers of
those who would depend only on their wits and efforts for worldly
success, on their character in misfortune, or on the doctor alone
in illness were always relatively small" (p. 32). In the absence
of this rationalistic approach, even talented people found it
difficult to sustain their intellectual effort and relapsed into their
old-fashioned Hinduism.

The plight of the Indian intellectual can be seen from the
fact that Indian society acknowledges greatness in religious
but not in intellectual matters. Chaudhuri rightly says that Hindu
society "understood religious greatness, particularly, in its mi-
raculous aspect, it also understood worldly greatness, but had no
consciousness of anything in-between, which belonged to the
spirit of man" (p. 35). In such a society, one needs courage to
pursue intellectual activity for its own sake. Conditions in India
are so pitiable that until recently, "the vocation of authorship
was a complete innovation, as also was the business of publishing" (p. 35). These activities have now started as a result of
the Westernized influence. But they have created a clash between
the Westernized intellectuals and the traditional Hindus. This
conflict of cultures has been further accentuated since Independence for political reasons.

IV   *Other Factors Disfavoring the Intellectual*

Another factor which Chaudhuri brings out in his analysis
of intellectual decline in India is education. Standards in education have been going down, and this invariably leads to the
decline of intellectual life. That India's intellectual life is in
decline may be seen from the fact that one cannot easily name
one dozen outstanding intellectuals in the whole country. And
yet the leading intellectuals of India like Jawaharlal Nehru, S.
Radhakrishnan, and Zakir Hussain were men of affairs. To get
away from the anti-intellectual atmosphere, India's brilliant
scientists like S. Chandrashekhar and Har Gobind Khorana have
settled in America.

Poverty is another main cause of intellectual backwardness, and while one cannot require the poor to eat well, Indian nutrition is seen by Chaudhuri as working against intellectual work: "In the first place, the food habits of the Indian middle-class and the kind of food they took, and still take, were utterly unsuited to give them the vitality and nervous energy needed for hard brainwork. The lack of adequate proteins was a particularly harmful factor" (p. 44). Poverty also encouraged the retention of the extended family which left time neither for leisure nor for introspection.

The situation is made worse by the fact that Hinduism does not encourage the development of individuality. Chaudhuri writes: "It is the authoritarian and intuitionist leanings of the Hindu mind which makes it unintellectual and sometimes positively anti-intellectual" (p. 46). The authority of the Vedas and the Upanishads is so supreme that a Hindu cannot believe in Socrates' dictum that an unexamined life is not worth living; nor can he begin to consider the philosophical doubt propounded by Descartes. The guru is not supposed to be criticized by his disciple. The result is that free enquiry and philosophical doubt are not traits encouraged among students.

Western technology has not brought with it Western science, so that Indian technicians have no culture. Chaudhuri points out: "To Indians in general, technology was a series of skills, which had nothing to do with the mental life of the users of technology" (p. 50). Thus, Indian scientists might believe in superstition, magic, and occult sources of knowledge. Lacking the broad humanistic culture of so many Western scientists, they often idle away their time watching third-rate movies, which have ousted every other form of imaginative entertainment.

Even the strong force that is Indian nationalism had no intellectual base. Indian history was largely conceived from the Hindu point of view, and there was more xenophobia and national egotism than scientific curiosity. Chaudhuri's criticism of Gandhism, tellingly expressed in his autobiography, is further elaborated in this book. He writes: "The Gandhian attitude towards morality and politics was a reaction from the intellectual to the intuitive standpoint congenial to the Hindu mind" (p. 53).

V *The Survival of the Indian Intellectual*

Chaudhuri, having survived for forty-seven years in such a difficult environment, wants younger intellectuals to profit from his experience. He informs the aspiring intellectual that he cannot survive by writing books alone, but should try his hand at journalism. As John Stuart Mill has put it: "The writings by which a man can live are not those that themselves live." Yet, the problem of livelihood cannot be ignored. Hence an aspiring intellectual should make himself fit for slow, unattractive toil.

Chaudhuri advises an Indian intellectual that if he can organize himself properly, he can turn out a good book every two years. If he is not able to do this, he should teach in universities or take a job in broadcasting. But an intellectual can survive only when he cultivates some important virtues: without intelligence, discipline, strength and determination, nothing is possible. Chaudhuri writes: "Success in intellectual life is a matter of inspiration, will-power, skill, and organization, and the organization must begin very early" (p. 60).

Such is the condition of Indian society that Chaudhuri has felt it necessary to describe the enemies of the Indian intellectual so that he can put himself on guard against them. Even in Indian universities, conditions are not propitious for intellectual effort: "The Indian academic world is laden with a deep somnolence without the justification of deep potations: it is mental vacuum, and not vintage port, which produces the abstracted air on the faces of the professors" (p. 64). During his visit to India, even an outsider on a brief visit like Edward Shils did not fail to notice this tendency everywhere: "The jealousy of an archaic head professor intimidates or obstructs the lively young man with ideas and enthusiasm, dull colleagues deaden the resonance of the atmosphere and contribute towards the slackening of standards."[8] It is hardly surprising therefore that brilliant young men find the Indian environment unusually dull. Either they suffer or they escape to more affluent countries like America or England.

But conditions are bad not only in universities but in Government service also. As in the former, so in the latter, the superiors suppress the talent of an aspiring intellectual. The very Hindu way of life breeds authoritarianism. Chaudhuri points out three ways in which superiors try to suppress the subordinates: "by insisting that every Government servant must take the permission of his superiors before publishing his writings; by trying to exercise censorship on them; and by demanding one-third of the earnings of an intellectual in Government service" (p. 67). Hence, Chaudhuri advises an aspiring intellectual that he should be secretive about his pursuits. If he tells others about his achievement, he will only invite envy. Indian society is so anti-intellectual that Chaudhuri advises his fellow-intellectual to have enough strength to be able to face his enemy. In addition, he should be indifferent toward money and careful in the selection of his marriage partner. It is only in this way that he can survive.

Concerning the practical side of an intellectual's life, Chaudhuri advises the production of wares that can sell. Hence Chaudhuri prefers English and American publishers because they can promote the sale of a book better and have a wider market than the Indian publishers. His advice ranges from the number of words a book should have to encouragement to be persistent even if ten publishers turn the book down. Chaudhuri prefers writers who grow books to writers who merely manufacture them. The former write their books under the pressure of the moment, while the latter merely write popular books on popular subjects.

From the above it is clear that Chaudhuri thinks of intellectuals as writers only. There is no reference to artists, painters, musicians, or sculptors as intellectuals in his book because he writes from his own experience. Chaudhuri narrows even this definition of intellectual to that of an Indian writing in English for he has a poor opinion of those writers who express themselves in the regional languages. Thus, he writes: "I have become convinced that books written in them [the Indian languages] do not make any impact which can be called intellectual. They serve as entertainment, of a high or low order, but many do not do even that, being very boring. Entertainment, I would add, is a legitimate and even indispensable part of writing, but, as entertainment pure and simple, it lies outside the scope of this discussion" (p. 72).

Chaudhuri advises Indian intellectuals to write on Indian themes and to formulate their ideas on the basis of their experience. They should write only about those things about 'which they feel deeply and sincerely. It is interesting to note that Chaudhuri has followed this advice in his own case. All his books are written on the basis of his Indian experience. Besides, he has an unusual mastery of English. He wants his fellow-intellectuals to cultivate mastery of English rhythms. To this end, he gives advice which is derived from his own experience:

. . . unless your English sounds like English, no British publisher will touch it. But comfort will perhaps be found in the fact that the range of English rhythms is so great and they themselves are so varied that an Indian will find that he has the advantage of a very wide margin of tolerance. The second assurance that I shall give the Indian writer is that to acquire the natural rhythm of English for writing, though not for speaking, it is not necessary to live among or mix with Englishmen. It is enough to be familiar with the sound of English prose in the works of a fairly large number of authors of different ages and epochs. (p. 80)

Chaudhuri followed this sound advice in his autobiography. He had never gone outside India, yet he showed an unusual technical mastery of English.

In spite of its practical utility, Chaudhuri's book is rather superficial. It does not deal with an important issue: the role of the intellectual in the changing society in India. Chaudhuri is brilliant in his analysis of the historical reasons for the plight of Indian intellectuals. He rightly says that the backwardness of Indian intellectuals is caused by a sense of economic insecurity. But mere survival of the Indian intellectual is a shallow point of view, intellectually. It is from this point of view that Edward Shils' book has greater depth and penetration. The range of Shils' book can be seen from the number of questions he has tried to answer in his book. Shils writes:

In a variety of ways the modern intellectuals of Asian and African countries have been "outsiders" *vis-à-vis* the ruling authorities, in tradition and in government. The question is: Can they become "insiders"? Can they, in other words, overcome their inheritance of distrust of constituted authority which came easily to them in the period of foreign rule? Can they take positive responsibility in the fields of opinion and political action? Can they come to feel fully at home in their own societies, and can they become creative with their materials which their own societies and their relations with other societies provide? Can they maintain a fruitful tension between incorporation into their own societies and their newly established systems of authority and the critical detachment and autonomy which are essential to the deeper life of the intellectual everywhere in all societies?[9]

If Chaudhuri had cared to raise and answer the questions posed above, his book would have been far more valuable. As it is, his book provides useful practical advice, but little relating to the deeper issues involving the Indian intellectual.

VI *Portrait of an Intellectual*

The case of Rabindra Nath Tagore provides an interesting instance of how an intellectual has to suffer in India. Chaudhuri has written two articles[10] on Tagore because his own suffering runs parallel to that of the great Nobel prize winner. Indians were as prejudiced against Tagore as they have been against Chaudhuri. Tagore also found his audience in the West, but Chaudhuri has gone one better and left India to settle in England. It has been the misfortune of many great Indians that they have been persecuted and hounded out of their own country by their countrymen. Both Tagore and Chaudhuri provide moving examples of this type of alienation.

Tagore's meteoric rise to fame in the West occurred in 1912. His fame subsequently declined by 1930. The reason for this eclipse is to be found in the mediocrity of the translations of Tagore's works. Indeed Chaudhuri has great praise for Tagore's original works: "In Bengali, Tagore's writing always shows as much strength as beauty, and never gives any impression of being pretty, euphuistic or jejune. In fact, to regard Tagore as pretty is as foolish as it would be to apply the term to Botticelli, Mozart or Keats."[11] His translations in English only show the poet in fancy dress.

Chaudhuri has made a brilliant psychological analysis of

Tagore's personality. He argues that when an introverted person tries to be an extrovert, there are harmful effects on personality. After being awarded the Nobel prize, Tagore, instead of continuing to write, tried to do many other things which did not belong to his proper vocation. He became something of a playboy, but his artificial cosmopolitanism made him belong neither to the East nor to the West, even when he tried to become a public figure as a one-man cultural delegation to Europe. Eventually, there was so much pose and pretense in the man, in Chaudhuri's view, that he tried to cultivate Indonesian ballet at Shantiniketan—his educational centre in Bengal.

By temperament, Tagore was rather unsocial and always felt alienated from his fellow-Indians. After his recognition in the West, he tried to abandon India altogether, which Chaudhuri analyzes as a big mistake: "His resentment against his people made him think that the Western recognition was going to be a compensation for him, that henceforth he could regard the Western world as his sphere of action and become an international moral influence. He could never become that, for what the West found in his writings was, in a manner of speaking, a sweetly scented room-freshener, for the stuffy atmosphere of its mental life before the first world war."[12] Indeed even Yeats and Rothenstein, who promoted Tagore in the West, became disillusioned with his artificial prettiness, and Tagore was stranded between East and West.

CHAPTER 7

Scholar Extraordinary

WHEN Chaudhuri came to write a book on Max Muller, he found a spirit congenial to his own self. There was in Muller's life the same struggle, the same suffering which Chaudhuri recorded so minutely in his autobiography. Muller was a self-made man. In his early days, he was so poor that he used to walk thirty-five miles to meet his mother. Chaudhuri's insight into the aspirations and sufferings of a scholar's life enabled him to give a brilliant portrait of Muller. So that *Scholar Extraordinary* is not only Muller but also Chaudhuri himself. Hence a biography of one by the other is bound to be of great interest to readers all over the world. Its size, scope, and thoroughness, added to the author's total involvement, both personally and in terms of ideas, make it fascinating as well as instructive.

Chaudhuri's biography makes an attempt to relate the personal history of Muller with the history of the whole period. It involves prodigious labor over a six-year period. The work shows patient enquiry into such diverse fields as the German Romantic movement, Christian theology, nineteenth-century church history, Sanskrit, and many others. In addition, it is a detailed study of Muller's enormous output. In order to re-create the milieu of his hero, Chaudhuri went to Oxford where Muller passed a large part of his life. This has enabled him to feel what Muller might have felt. Added to this, there is minute attention to every detail. Every letter or diary has been consulted. The result is a painstaking piece of research.

The reason why Chaudhuri got interested in Muller is that he has always been interested in the discovery of India by the Western Orientalists, and Muller's contribution to Indology is outstanding. It is surprising that Muller never visited India, yet he is the discoverer of the glory that was ancient India. Swami

Vivekananda paid Muller the highest tribute when he wrote that Muller lived and moved "in the world of Indian thought for fifty years or more, and watched the sharp inter-change of light and shade in the interminable forest of Sanskrit literature with deep interest and heartfelt love till they have all sunk into his very soul and coloured his whole being."[1]

Chaudhuri has unusual sympathy for German scholars in general, as may be seen from his reverential attitude toward Mommsen in *The Continent of Circe*. He has even greater regard for Muller because he combined in himself the best traits of English, French, and German scholarship. Muller spent his early days in Germany; subsequently he stayed for some time in Paris; later, he settled at Oxford. Because he was a German expatriate in England, most of his writings are in English. It is for this reason that Chaudhuri spent six years in Oxford hunting through the archives of the Bodleian Library. The result of all this is an authoritative life of a scholar of the glorious Sanskrit heritage.

Chaudhuri's biography suffers from the defect of hero worship. Thus, there are certain details given which are unlikely to interest anyone. These details are inevitable, however, since the author has chosen to write a biography in the literal sense of the word, with emphasis on the life of the man rather than on evaluation of his work. For instance, Chaudhuri tells us how Muller came to write the translation of the *Rig-Veda*, but nothing about the authenticity of the translation. The level of the biography is all the more unfortunate in that Mrs. Max Muller, in her two-volume biography of her husband, had already described his life competently.[2] This information is supplemented by Muller's own *Auld Lang Syne*[3] and his autobiography.[4] With so much material of this sort already available, Chaudhuri's work makes dull reading in parts. Chaudhuri has only shaken the ghost of a great scholar.

I   *Superiority of the Scholarly Life*

Max Muller is remembered in India because he was a great admirer of Hindu civilization and spirituality. It is because of his initial interest that other Germans won renown as the discovers of the Sanskrit heritage. In present-day India all the cultural centers of Germany are known as Max Muller Bhawans, but even in the nineteenth century, there is documentation of the emotions he aroused, as may be seen by the following touching letter to him:

Most respected Sir, Sunday was the mail day, on which English mail letters are delivered at Madras. That morning, while I was eagerly expecting the postman, he gave me a card received from you, in which the following lines were written: 'Professor Max Muller is seriously ill and not able to attend to any letters.' When I saw these lines tears trickled down my cheeks unconsciously. When I showed the card to my friends who spend the last days of their life like mine in reading the Bhagavatgitha and some such religious books, they were also very much overpowered with grief. (p. 4)

If this letter is any indication, Muller seems to have enjoyed great prestige in India when he was alive.

Because both scholars showed how ideas can influence action, Chaudhuri compares Muller to Karl Marx. Muller was a man speaking to men, not a scholar gypsy. His life showed that "ideas do travel from the scholar's study over the wide world of the mind" (p. 8), so that even when he wrote on a specialized subject like the Vedas, his approach was general and popular. Chaudhuri is very much impressed by this aspect of Muller's personality.

But Chaudhuri places unnecessary emphasis on the life of a scholar-thinker as superior to that of others. He believes that his own life, which is dedicated to scholarship, is superior to the lives of others and that worldly success is unimportant as a measure of a person's worth. He then develops this point to argue that those who create confusion between the life of thought and the life of action lead a futile life. Thus, Chaudhuri would say that the lives of Gandhi, Nehru, and Tagore ended as "ghastly tragedies" (p. 9). These personal views in the life of Muller are as irrelevant as the portraits of Oxford dons like Mark Pattison and Benjamin Jowett who occupy so much un-called for space in his book.

II *Early Days*

Chaudhuri describes Muller's early days in Dessau, Leipzig, Berlin, and Paris in light but masterful touches. Muller was not

born in a rich family. His father died when Muller was four. Subsequently he took on the responsibility for his mother. It is for
this reason that his letters to his mother are so emotional.

In his early days, Muller was devoted to music. He learned
the piano secretly and became friendly with Mendelsohn. Among
contemporary composers, he not only liked Mendelsohn's ex-
uberance but was also a great admirer of Liszt's virtuosity and
Schumann's lyricism. He was interested in the what rather
than the how of music. He loved the simplicity of the harpsichord,
hence he liked Haydn and Mozart. This rich musical culture
earned him a great reputation as a pianist at Oxford.

If music was Muller's love during his school days, literature
became his passion during his college days. From his early days,
he became interested in India because of his love of Sanskrit
literature. After completing his doctorate in eighteen months at
the incredible age of twenty, in 1844, at the age of twenty-one,
he translated the *Hitopdesa*—the oldest collection of Indian
fables. Besides Sanskrit, he was deeply interested in Persian
which Ruckert had taught him. After his early days in Germany,
Muller spent a difficult time in Paris, where he enjoyed his
pleasant independence but had no money. It was here that he
came under the influence of Bunsen who was a brilliant teacher
of Sanskrit.

The essential interest of Chaudhuri's biography lies in the
fact that he presents some eternal reflections on life in his subject.
The method employed in this case is the same which Chaudhuri
employed in his autobiography. Muller remained a devoted
scholar whether he was in Leipzig, Paris, or London. Chaudhuri
uses a musical metaphor to explain the significance of a scholar's
life:

The unity of such lives is that of harmonic and contrapuntal music.
The basic strand in it is always the deep bass of the early environment, punctuating the other melodic lines and sometimes surging
above them. Then comes the middle register of work and workaday
life, and, above all, there is the treble line of creative moods and
moments of revelation, all accompanied by trills and other decorative
figures of sense experience. Such a life is no more ill-organised than
a symphony. (p. 48)

A significant event that took place in Muller's early life was his meeting with Dwarkanath Tagore who was staying in Paris. Tagore was familiar with both Indian and Western music and introduced Muller to the glory of Indian music. At first, Muller could perceive neither rhythm, nor melody, nor harmony in Indian music. But Tagore told him that he had felt the same way about Western music when he heard it for the first time, but he had persisted and finally understood the grandeur of Western music. He told Muller that he would discover the rich melody and intricate rhythm of Indian music if he continued to hear it many times. Thus, Dwarkanath Tagore was the first person to plead for Indian music in the West—a work which has been subsequently carried out by Ravi Shankar and Yehudi Menuhin. Tagore's advice had a profound effect on Muller. As a result of this encounter, Muller not only aspired for a cultural synthesis between the East and the West but also remained in touch with Indian nationalism throughout his life.

In his early days of struggle in Paris, Muller was helped by Burnouf and Bunsen—particularly the latter who introduced him to the glory of the Vedas. At that time, the world of Oriental scholarship was unexplored territory. With so much to discover, Muller felt like Keats: "Then felt I like some watcher of the skies/ When a new planet swims into his ken."[5] It was with Bunsen's support that Muller was able to complete the translation of the *Rig-Veda*, which was published by the East India Company which wanted to show a genuine interest in India's art and literature rather than exploitation.

While Muller was in England, he cared more for his vocation than for his profession. His strong sense of devotion to Sanskrit can be seen from the cheerfulness with which he put up with his poverty. The reason why Chaudhuri's biography makes such fascinating reading is that he found his own prototype in Muller. Both scholars suffered extreme poverty in their life, yet they lived for their ideal. What Chaudhuri says about Muller is also true about himself. "Certainly, it is the most difficult thing in life to make vocation and profession merge. Max Muller had arrived at the starting-point of that process without achieving finality" (p. 65).

Muller's ambition, in his early days, was to do something

original. He never visited India, but he was so much fascinated by the picture of Benares that he took up the study of Sanskrit seriously. Thereafter, he mentally lived in India. It was sheer inspiration which made Muller put the *Rig-Veda* side by side with Kant's *Critique of Pure Reason*. Muller writes: "The bridge of thoughts and sighs that spans the whole history of the Aryan world has its first arch in the *Vedas,* its last in Kant's *Critique.* While in the *Veda* we may study the childhood, we may study in Kant's *Critique of Pure Reason* the perfect manhood of the Aryan mind" (p. 90). It is to Muller's credit that he could perceive the resemblance between such disparate works and treat them as the expression of the Ayran spirit. It was this sense of relationship between East and West which made Muller concentrate on the study of the early growth of the Aryan mind.

III *Oxford*

It is characteristic of Chaudhuri that he gives precedence to environment over the individual. As in his autobiography, so here, he is interested more in cultural history than the history of the individual. Muller came to Oxford at the age of twenty-five and stayed on there till his death at the age of seventy-seven. During this long stay, he made Oxford as much as Oxford made him. It was here that Muller cultivated his main interests— theology, comparative philology, Sanskrit, and music. If he was something of a classical scholar in Paris, he became once again a student at Oxford.

Oxford was valuable to Muller because it allowed his vocation and profession to merge. As a German expatriate, he faced many troubles, but his scholarship in Sanskrit won him jobs of various sorts. In 1854, he was given a professorship which provided him with a sense of security. Henceforth, he yearned for a quiet village in Germany or a forest retreat in India, but he never left Oxford. Muller's advice was much sought after because it helped in the understanding of the oldest Indian literature, philosophy, and religion. It is paradoxical that by making the Vedas popular, Muller helped not only the cause of British rule in India but also the cause of Indian nationalism.

Chaudhuri's portrait of Oxford shows that in the nineteenth

century, Oxford was not very different from Indian universities of today. Muller suffered from being a foreigner. Moreover, since he had to depend on Oxford for money and his position, "he could not hope to be entirely free of its intrigues, rivalries, antipathies and partisanship" (p. 219). While Oxford provided him with certain well-deserved honors, it also gave him some heart-breaking disappointments. Thus, in 1858, he was elected a Fellow of All Souls, a rare honor for a foreigner. But this was followed by his failure to get the Boden professorship. Chaudhuri provides a description of the competition and controversy that took place between Muller and Monier Williams for the privileged post and points out that "the election to the Professorship had the character of a parliamentary election, and the candidates followed the same methods in contesting for the post" (p. 221). After a hot campaign, Williams was elected for the post by a narrow margin of one hundred votes.

Many voted for Williams because they believed his election would help the diffusion of Christianity in India. Moreover, it was argued that Muller's field of specialization—the Vedas—had only an archaeological interest, whereas Williams was interested in the live Sanskrit literature of a later day and would be more useful as a guide to the Hindu mind. On the personal level, Muller was accused of not being an Englishman; of not being able to write English well; and of being irreligious. His defeat on personal, political, and religious grounds continued to rankle in his mind, more so because as a Sanskrit scholar, he enjoyed worldwide popularity. Chaudhuri's description hardly does any credit to the academic life at Oxford.

Muller's inability to get the Boden professorship was partly mitigated by the fact that in 1865, he was able to get the post of Oriental Sub-Librarian at the Bodleian. Eight years later, Muller realized that he owed greater duty to Sanskrit scholarship than to comparative philology and in 1875 resigned from this post so that he could devote his mature years to the study of Sanskrit. The university did not want to have the embarassment of losing his services, so he was provided with a deputy who was to get half his salary and discharge Muller's duties as professor in comparative philology. Thus Muller could devote himself entirely to the cause of Sanskrit scholarship.

IV *Muller the Man*

Chaudhuri devotes a great deal of space to love, courtship, and marriage in the life of Muller. From his description, Muller emerges as a patient lover, a doting husband, and a devoted father. However, Muller as a lover is given an inordinate amount of space. His courtship of Beata Georgina, whom he met in 1853, is described at length, especially through profuse quotations from the journal of the scholar's beloved. Chaudhuri's elaborate description of Muller's love story reminds one of Auden's lines: "Some of the latest researchers even say/ Love made him weep his pints like you and me."[6] Certainly, the fact that a German specialist in Sanskrit and comparative philology took seven years to marry an English girl belonging to fashionable society has only a marginal interest, but Chaudhuri takes thirty pages to describe the love story of Muller.

Throughout *Scholar Extraordinary* there are general comments on the Victorian attitude toward love. Since Muller was a religious man for whom marriage was a sacrament, such comments as the following are irrelevant and serve only to display Chaudhuri's familiarity with English cultural history: " . . . while the Hindu or the Muslim polygamist uses a number of women as notes in a simultaneously sounded chord, the modern Western polygamists play them *arpeggio*, making marriage very much a matter of sexual convenience" (p. 148). In another generalization on the same subject he says: "The Victorians succeeded in a very great measure in reconciling the intensity of love with its concentration on one object." This sweeping statement is immediately followed by yet another hasty generalization: "The Victorians were stodgy in their moralising but not in their love-making" (p. 151). The tone is similar to the many prurient statements in *The Continent of Circe*.

V *The Discovery of Ancient India*

Muller discovered the heritage of India when India was not a free country and restored the faith of Indians in their great cultural achievement. In doing so, he avoided the Romantic enthusiasm of some German scholars as well as the extreme antipathy of some Englishmen. He showed the greatness of the

Vedas to the shallow dabblers in Indian spirituality and wanted to show that "Schopenhauer was wrong when in a discussion at Frankfurt, he told him that the Upanishads was the only important portion of the Veda that deserved to be studied, the rest was nothing but priestly rubbish."[7] It was through Muller's persistent effort that the Vedas have earned their well-deserved importance in the West.

So great was Muller's attachment to ancient India that he transformed his own name into Sanskrit. It was wrongly believed in India that the Pandits of Benares gave Max Muller the Sanskrit name "Moksha Mulara." Chaudhuri points out that it was Muller himself who transformed his own name into Sanskrit (p. 140). He did so because he had great regard for ancient India. Expressing his deep sense of gratitude to the sages and the poets of ancient India, Muller said: "They have revealed to me a whole world of thought of which no trace existed anywhere else, and they helped me to throw the first faint rays of light and reason on the darkest period in the history of religion, philosophy, and mythology."[8]

Muller's knowledge of India was derived from his contacts with distinguished Indians. He was singularly lucky in meeting many talented Indians of his day. Among these, the prominent ones were Dwarkanath Tagore, Raja Radhakant Deb, Debendranath Tagore, Keshab Chandra Sen, Rajendralal Mitra, Bhao Daji and Behramji Malabari. His regard for great Indian personalities found eloquent expression in what he wrote in 1899: "What I feel and what I wish my friends would feel with me, is that a country which, even in these unheroic days, could produce a Raja Rammohan Roy, a Keshab Chandra Sen, a Behramji Malabari and a Ramabai, is not a decadent country, but may look forward to bright sunny future, as it can look back with satisfaction and even pride on four thousand years of a not inglorious history."[9] Muller was particularly friendly with Keshab Chandra Sen who was a daring social and religious reformer of his time. Among Indian women, Muller knew two particularly well—Ramabai and Anandibai Joshi. Through them, he tried to raise the status of women in India. There is one surprising omission in Chaudhuri's account. He fails to mention a most distinguished Indian—Swami Vivekananda—whom Muller met a few times. Both had great admiration and regard for each other.

So great was Muller's love for India that he regarded the ancient Indian civilization as the best in the whole world. At a time when Englishmen had a certain hostility toward Indians, Muller had the courage to make the following remarkable pronouncement in his Cambridge lectures, *India: What Can It Teach Us* (1882):

If I were asked under what sky the human mind has most fully developed some of its choicest gifts, has most deeply pondered on the greatest problems of life, and has found solutions of some of them which well deserve the attention even of those who have studied Plato and Kant—I should point to India. And if I were to ask myself from what literature we, here in Europe, we who have been nurtured almost exclusively on the thoughts of Greeks and Romans, and of one semitic race, the Jewish, may draw that corrective which is most wanted in order to make our inner life more perfect, more comprehensive, more universal, in fact more truly human, a life, not for this life only, but a transfigured and eternal life—again I should point to India. (p. 303)

This tribute is remarkable because it came at a time when India was thoroughly demoralized under British rule. Muller went on to argue that the Hindus had been subsequently spoiled by Muslim and British domination.

Muller never ignored the practical side of his scholarship. He hoped that his edition of the *Rig-Veda* would have a beneficial effect on the practical life of the Hindus. It is interesting to note that his discoveries in comparative philology gave rise to the idea of Indian nationalism. It showed the importance that Sanskrit occupied in relation to other Indo-Germanic languages. Muller went to the extent of saying that "a comparative philologist without a knowledge of Sanskrit was like an astronomer without a knowledge of mathematics" (p. 313). Muller made the Hindus realize that they had a glorious past and a rich heritage which should make them proud of their civilization.

Muller was interested in the serious aspects of Hinduism. He had no liking for the orgiastic or erotic aspects of Hinduism which have been so much glorified in the West recently. But it is surprising to note that Muller showed as much concern for

Hinduism as for Christianity. Nevertheless he wanted to use his prestige as a Sanskrit scholar for the purpose of spreading Christianity in India, and it was partly under his influence that some educated Indians took to Christianity.

In spite of his regard for Christianity, Muller maintained a highly rationalistic approach toward the Vedas. He was very critical of those Indians who believed that all scientific knowledge was to be found in the Vedas, since he did not agree with the view that the Vedas had a divine origin. Muller was particularly critical of Swami Dayanand Saraswati who said: "All wisdom was to be found in it [the Veda] down to the discovery of the power of steam and its application to steam engines for railways."[10] This disagreement aside, Muller valued Dayanand Saraswati's contribution toward religious and social reform and praised him for the courage he exhibited in championing the cause of widow remarriage, and in denouncing idolatry, polytheism, and the caste system.

Muller himself made a substantial contribution toward social reform in India. He was concerned about widows and pleaded that their burning after their husband's death should be stopped. In the same way, he wanted child marriage to be abolished in India and recommended that the age of consent, in the case of women, should be raised to sixteen. Thus, even in his time, Muller enjoyed a reputation in India as much for his Sanskrit scholarship as for his concern for social reform.

Muller's attitude toward the British in India was that British rule was providential and Indians would get freedom only when they were mature enough for it. Yet, he was aware that certain British administrators misused their authority in India. Muller was particularly courageous in championing the cause of the nationalist Bal Gandadhar Tilak whose Sanskrit scholarship he appreciated. Walking this fine line, Muller is praised by Chaudhari for "his balance of mind and capacity to see both sides of any question. He could thus support British rule in India and also champion India and Indians" (p. 343).

VI   *Language, Religion, and Mythology*

Max Muller was a pioneer in various fields of human knowledge. Among these, the most important was language. Chaudhuri devotes one full chapter to Muller's contribution to the science of language. This part of his book is not as interesting as other parts because Muller's theory of language seems outmoded now. Yet, it has a historical importance. Muller was particularly interested in the relationship between language and thought. For this reason, he regarded language as "the autobiography of the human mind" (p. 179). He uses an analogy from geology to explain the growth of language. He believed in "the early development of language from the isolating stage to the agglutinative, and again from the agglutinative to the inflective" (p. 186). In this way, he applied the theory of evolution to the science of language. In these days, Muller's faith in philology has been superseded by our faith in semantics, but Chaudhuri gives great importance to Muller's contribution in this field.

Besides his work on language, Muller devoted the third stage of his life—which Chaudhuri calls "Vanaprastha" in a chapter by that name—to the study of religion and mythology. Muller had such prodigious energy that in his old age he undertook the tremendous task of editing the forty-nine volumes of *The Sacred Books of the East*. These books are remarkable not only for their critical, but also historical, study of Eastern religions. This vast project was followed by his brilliant Gifford lectures on religion, wherein "he presented a stupendous synthesis of the evolution of religion in an ascending process in four stages, which he called Natural Religion, Physical Religion, Anthropological Religion and Theosophy or Psychological Religion" (p. 361). Though Chaudhuri gives great importance to Muller's work on language, it is as a thinker on religion that Muller is still read.

Muller's interest in mythology ran parallel to his interest in religion and language. Chaudhuri points out: "For Max Muller mythology, language and religion were cognate subjects. In fact, his excursion into mythology was an extension of his work on language . . ." (p. 362). Muller tried to find reason behind the unreason and fantasy of mythology. In mythology, he tried to explore the prehistory of the human mind in the same way as he had through the medium of language. It is to Chaudhuri's credit that he presents a clear and simple analysis of Muller's contribution to these abstruse branches of human thought.

VII   *Chaudhuri as a Biographer*

Chaudhuri has great admiration for Muller. For this reason, he defends him persuasively against all his detractors. One sometimes feels that Chaudhuri is partial toward his hero, though he states the opposite point of view also. The fact is that on the whole, this book surprises everyone, given Chaudhuri's previous works, because of its reserved and objective tone. Nissim Ezekiel makes a good appraisal:

Those who are acquainted with Chaudhuri's earlier writings, where evidence is often ignored or distorted if it goes against his central arguments, must give him credit this time for restraining his dogmatic and polemical tendencies. He seems to have accepted his role as biographer and cultural historian with little or none of that ruthless prejudice which served him so well in shaping his dissenter's view of Indian life and history.[11]

If Chaudhuri was rather slavish in his attitude in *A Passage to England,* here he sets himself up as an authority on Great Britain. His long stay in England seems to have given him some unusual insights into English life. For this reason, he makes too many sweeping generalizations about the Victorian age. The story of Muller's courting of Georgina Grenfell, whom he eventually married, is told with some ideological moralizing on Victorian Romanticism in contrast to that of the twentieth century. The following quotation shows that Chaudhuri's strong convictions are not always convincing:

The episode shows how superficial, untrue and malicious was the later running-down of the Victorians as stodgy, insensitive and snobbish people. On the contrary, they had not undergone that erosion of the passionate side of the human personality which has certainly come about today, passion and sensuality not being exchangeable terms. Only, the great Victorians knew that passion brought in its wake suffering just as it also did exultant happiness. The suffering they tried to bear with stoicism and in silence, a type of behaviour not accessible to cleverness. But even worldly Victorians could sense the stoicism and respect it. The Grenfells did not sneer at Muller because without possessing money he had aspired after their daughter. Their worldliness could go with an appreciation of unworldliness. (p. 119)

What Chaudhuri says about the Victorian age is perhaps also true about our own time. If one quoted a twentieth-century example comparable to the episode Chaudhuri cites, he would not accept it as a reliable proof that "an erosion of the passionate side has not taken place." There must be as many people today as in the Victorian age who know that "passion brought in its wake suffering . . . ," etc. Such suffering is surely borne "with stoicism and silence" by as many moderns as it was by the Victorians. And worldliness going with an appreciation of unworldliness is by no means unknown in our time. But many of Chaudhuri's invidious comparisons only reveal that he is unnecessarily pleading for the Victorian age.

Chaudhuri is usually a very controversial writer, but in his Muller's biography, he has written only one chapter which contains polemics. This exciting chapter deals with Muller's political and intellectual actions, properly so-called. "He felt that it was his duty," Chaudhuri points out, "to support the side which he believed to be right, and in committing himself to a cause he showed neither timidity nor half-heartedness, though this brought him more than a controversialist's share of abuse" (p. 239). Chaudhuri describes these controversies at length but ends on an unexpected note: "scholars themselves should avoid them, and the layman should ignore them" (p. 264). This is a very strange statement from a man who has written the largest number of abrasive and controversial articles in India. But old age seems to have matured him. Even when an entire review of A *Passage to England* spoke of the book in terms of a dog wagging its tail, Chaudhuri sadly noted the fact but made no attempt to counter the critic's charge. In a recent article, he merely said that he had sincerely tried to praise a foreign culture but had been thoroughly misunderstood. I had better quote Chaudhuri's apology in his own words: "I had, of course, committed an unforgivable offence against the code of Hindu ethics in respect of foreigners—I had praised a foreign culture with sincerity, which no Hindu is allowed to do. Interested praise of foreign nations is a different matter."[12]

But these polemics apart, Chaudhuri places great emphasis on the human side of Muller's personality. In the chapter entitled "Life, Love and Death," Chaudhuri provides an elaborate description of Muller as a father. He talks about Muller's morbid preoccupation with death and the fact that he was never the same person after the death of his eldest daughter, Ada. Muller's personal diary is quoted to show his habit of self-analysis and his torment over his dead daughter. Such conflicts fill the pages of the diaries of many unhappy souls and give little insight into the connection between the man and his ideas.

Chaudhuri emphasizes the human side of Muller's personality because he wants to stress that he was more of an intellectual than a scholar. Muller's purpose was to understand the world around him and influence the lives of his fellowmen. Thus, Chaudhuri writes of Muller as "less a scholar in the strict sense of the word than an intellectual, and the difference is basic" (p. 265).

The great achievement of Muller lies in the fact that he was entirely a self-made man. A real disciple of Kant, he led a scholarly life of categorical imperatives. In accordance with a distinction made by Nietzsche, Chaudhuri divides thinkers into two categories—Apollonian and Dionysian. Muller belonged to the former category because he wanted "to reduce experience to order, and present even the supra-rational as rational, or at any rate in a form which would be accessible to human intelligence" (p. 378). It was due to this factor that Muller was able to treat ancient religions scientifically. His lifelong dedication to learning made him a pioneer and explorer in the fields of Indology, religion, language and mythology. Chaudhuri's biography of this remarkable man reveals the best in Muller's personality and thought. In so doing, Chaudhuri also reveals all that is best in his own personality and thought.

CHAPTER 8

Conclusion

NIRAD C. Chaudhuri is one of those rare intellectuals who forgo the safety of a regular salary and dedicate themselves entirely to the pursuit of learning. With exceptional courage, he has made intellectual writing his main vocation. He has occasionally taken jobs, but, with all the economic hardships, he has not lost faith in his lofty pursuit. Ever since he wrote the controversial dedication to his autobiography, he has been unpopular with the Indian administration. The dedication read: "to the memory of the British Empire in India which conferred subjecthood on us but withheld citizenship." But in spite of this tyranny of the foreign domination, "all that was good and living within us was made, shaped, and quickened by the same British rule."

The paradox contained in this dedication has been characteristic of the entire intellectual output of Chaudhuri. In a way, all his six books are variations on one theme—India's encounter with the West. His entire work has been the most authentic account of the credit and the debit side of the clash that took place between Indian and Western civilization as a result of British rule. Chaudhuri is an inveterate anglophile, but he has made it his passion to enquire into the moorings of the Hindu way of life against the background of the Western way of life.

In his early days, Chaudhuri grew up in an atmosphere of moral awareness in which Christian-European ethics continually confronted the Hindu view of morality. It is this fascinating dialectic which is responsible for Chaudhuri's strong attack on Hinduism. He once said: "It [Hinduism] has discovered an intimate connection between vice and animal protein, but has no inkling of the connexion between that organic product and the more positive virtues."[1] Chaudhuri rightly believes that without vitality and will-power, human potentialities cannot be realized to their maximum extent. His plea for nonvegetarianism

arises from his Westernized attitude toward life. He is an unusual Hindu who fell so much in love with the West that subsequently, he went and settled in England. It is only in that
alien environment that he has been able to realize his intellectual
potentialities in the best possible way.

Chaudhuri writes in his autobiography that during his post-
graduation days he got so lost in the labyrinth of learning that
he started reading the *Encyclopaedia Brittanica* with avid interest. Ever since he has been a dedicated intellectual. It is
natural to have great expectations from such a lofty soul. But
Chaudhuri belied them. He started as a brilliant journalist, but
he could not organize his material beyond small articles. It is
for this reason that his first book appeared when he was fifty-one.
Even this work suffers from a lack of structure. Chaudhuri's
second book—a travelogue—appeared when he was sixty, while
his third book, in which he wrote the harshest criticism of India,
was written at the age of sixty-eight. His subsequent three works
have appeared in his seventies. Meanwhile, at the age of seventy-
eight, he has planned a stimulating work on Hinduism.[2]

Chaudhuri has never been a professor himself, but he resembles
Indian professors in at least one way. In the case of the latter,
their first book is invariably their most important and usually
their only work. In the same way, Chaudhuri's *Autobiography*
was his *magnum opus*. All his major themes were announced in
this book, merely to be elaborated subsequently. In the later
books, he not only served old wine in not very new bottles but
came nowhere near the greatness of his earlier work. The im-
mensely erudite autobiography was written in a state of deep
turmoil born out of the inner tension created by the consciousness of the wide chasm between what W. B. Yeats called the
"race/ And the reality."[3] Chaudhuri could not bear what seemed
to him to be the deep degradation of the once-glorious Hindu
race because his norms were borrowed from the West.

In Chaudhuri's first work, one sees the Romantic attitudinizing
of an angry old man narrating the story of his maladjustment.
He has never been able to adjust to the Indian environment, and
has always critically analyzed every aspect of Hindu society
from the Western point of view. The most moving part of his
autobiography is the severe satire written with Swiftian bitter-

ness on the once-glorious Hindu civilization that had lost its moorings and undergone a slow and painful decay since 1192—the time, when according to Chaudhuri, the Muslim cycle of Indian history started. Few Indian writers have described this degeneration of Hindu society as well as Chaudhuri has done.

Chaudhuri's great achievement in his autobiography was that he projected his own inner conflict as the conflict of the whole race. By a brilliant depth analysis of his own attitudes, he saw in his own microcosm the macrocosm of the whole Hindu ethos. But in spite of Chaudhuri's brilliant analysis of Indian nationalism, he let his countrymen down. The very cause—the resurgence of Hindu society—which was so dear to his heart, could not be served because of the tone of his book which is so obviously addressed to the Western reader. His desire to please Western readers can be seen even in details such as the fact that whereas every quotation in Latin and French is left untranslated, every couplet in Sanskrit is rendered into English.

Chaudhuri's second book, *A Passage to England*, is brilliantly written. His enthusiasm for Western music and European art seems to have inspired a bright English style, but he makes observations on many aspects of English life which only an Indian could have discovered. For example, he notes that Englishmen keep the interior of their houses rich because they find the weather outside dull; he makes shrewd comments on the difference of light and temperature, mentioning that he felt it was early morning or early evening all the time. Yet Chaudhuri's book was not liked in India, for in order to please Englishmen, Chaudhuri compared the Indians unfavorably with the English in almost all cases: he found that the amateurs at a certain club in England painted better than some professionals in India; he liked the reserve of Englishmen because it helped them preserve their energy for work. Along with these comments, he implied that Indians do not work hard and therefore should not lose the pleasure of talking.[4] If Chaudhuri had avoided these invidious comparisons, his book would have been appreciated not only in England but in India also.

Chaudhuri's third book, *The Continent of Circe*, expresses his complete disillusionment with India. The major part of the book deals with the Hindus, but nowhere, in about 150 pages, does he have one kind word to say about them. In this book, Chaudhuri has been influenced by Toynbee's historical philosophy. In light of this philosophy he maintains that the Hindus had failed to surmount the challenge of their hostile physical and human environment. Hence they lapsed into a mixture of religious asceticism and a fatalistic acceptance of dirt, squalor, and disorder.

Chaudhuri's disillusionment with India is partly caused by his own maladjustment. He has noted in a recent article: "In the streets, urchins stare at me and shout from behind: 'Johnnie Walker, Passing Show, Charlie Chaplin,' "5 In *The Continent of Circe,* he has explicitly said: "I never forget that my ways are utterly inconsistent with the spirit of the milieu and with the culture shaped by it. . . ."6 Thus, much of Chaudhuri's criticism of India arises from purely personal reasons. Yet, no one has expressed his dissatisfaction with his own country as brilliantly and as venomously as Chaudhuri has done.

Chaudhuri's next two books *To Live or Not to Live* and *The Intellectual in India* have been widely read with admiration in India. His fourth book *To Live or Not to Live* contains some useful criticism of Indian society and makes a brilliant plea for its modernization. Chaudhuri is a brilliant critic of Indian norms and mores and the style of this book is scathing and polemical. He is ruthlessly candid and provocative, and no serious discussion of Indian social problems can afford to ignore the ideas contained in this book.

In his fifth book, *The Intellectual in India,* Chaudhuri wants his fellow-intellectuals to profit from his experience. As he has said: "The intellectual insolvency and the economic insolvency of the middle-class have been running along parallel course during the last thirty years, each keeping pace with the other and helping each other."7 He has suffered the stupidities of Indian society and does not want another to undergo the same suffering. Hence, for any talented writer, this is a book of immense value.

Chaudhuri's latest work, *Scholar Extraordinary,* is a brilliant biography of Max Muller. There are several reasons why Chaudhuri's biography makes such a fascinating reading. First, like his biographer, Muller was also a poverty-stricken scholar with

slight aristocratic connections. Second, both Muller and Chaudhuri have shown a rare sense of dedication to the chosen vocation of a scholar. Third, Chaudhuri's keen interest in Western
music found in Muller a pianist who was always in demand at
Oxford gatherings. Both Muller and Chaudhuri have undertaken
a long mental voyage which is free from any dogma and which
is characterized by a disinterested pursuit of knowledge. Like
Chaudhuri, Muller had a great mastery of English style and he
wrote singularly smooth prose. Like Muller, Chaudhuri has a
dislike for the introverted scholasticism of the twentieth century
and has a passion for making a substantial contribution to the
commonly shared general intellectual culture. But in spite of
their dedication to the life of scholarship, both intellectuals
have a sneaking admiration for worldly success. For all these
reasons, Chaudhuri's biography of Muller makes fascinating
reading.

Chaudhuri's work shows the same mental energy and loquacity
which was characteristic of Muller himself. Muller's valuable
contribution lies in the fact that he made Europe conscious of
the stern and noble primitivism of the ancient Indian society
depicted in the *Rig-Veda*. It is through these spiritual values that
India can fertilize the religious life of the West. Side by side
with Muller's contribution to the history of ideas, Chaudhuri
talks about his personal life. Thus, he uses the scholar's marriage
not only as an occasion to generalize about the Victorian attitude
toward sex but also to point a moral. Chaudhuri says that the
spiritualized monogamous ideal thus belongs to Western culture
at its peak in the mid-Victorian age, when it combined the
German Romantic Movement with the Lutheran sacramentaliza-
tion of sex. As far as Muller's old age is concerned, Chaudhuri
reads some Indian notions into the life of his hero. Muller's
last days, when his daughter died in 1876, remind Chaudhuri of
a Hindu beaten into submission to his environment. In a shrewd
comment, Eric Stokes perceives the subtle relationship between
The Continent of Circe and *Scholar Extraordinary*. Mr. Stokes
writes: "That the close pursuit of the discipline of biography,
like that of history, should end in the demonstration that life is
more obdurate than we expected carries its own moral. *The
Continent of Circe* was Mr. Chaudhuri's fantasy; here the fan-

tasy is put up against living reality. The result is an unusual and remarkable biography by an unusual and remarkable man."[8] The tribute is richly deserved. Chaudhuri spent six years in writing the life of Muller. Few scholars can show the intellectual sweep, catholicity, and versatility which Chaudhuri has shown in this brilliant biography.

Chaudhuri's articles have been as important as his books.[9] In his articles he appears as a shrewd social and political commentator of the current scene in India. For instance, Chaudhuri has been very critical of India's dependence on the West. In a recent article, he explains this servile attitude in terms of India's pseudo-nationalism:

The Indian attitude towards foreign aid is equally the product of historical experience and of the nationalism shaped by it. India expects this aid as a matter of right and not as a favour, for reasons which are very cogent to the Indian people. They have been taught to attribute their poverty and economic backwardness to British exploitation, which was a part of Western imperialism. So the whole of the West is expected to pay reparations without any claim to gratitude.[10]

In this way, just as many saints survive on the generosity of wealthy people, so spiritual India survives on the generosity of the West. This parallel can be further elaborated in sociological terms. In Indian extended families, the lazy and the clever members survive on those who are sincere and hard-working; in the same way, India occupies the same position relative to the Western powers in the world family.

Thus Chaudhuri appears in the Indian intellectual ethos as a great dissenter who is a force to reckon with. All his articles in India's leading journals have been widely commented upon. As a satirist, he has few equals among Indo-Anglian writers. As a popular writer, he is full of quizzical witticisms. As a senior intellectual, he very often appears in the role of a sardonic moralist. His vigorous and volatile personality has gained him a wide audience in the West. This is a remarkable achievement considering the fact that he could not pass his M. A. and therefore could not be a professional academician. He suffered poverty and want for the major part of his life and worked in the unfertile Indian environment where encouragement is not

easily forthcoming. But through sheer courage, Chaudhuri over-
came all these hardships. Through sustained effort spread over
a large number of years, Chaudhuri is at present the leading
writer of nonfictional prose in India.

I *Critical Reaction*

It is a paradox that while Chaudhuri has so many admirers in
the West, he has a great many detractors in India. Since Chaudhuri has written mostly for Western readers, this fact has
irritated his sensitive Indian readers. Naturally, Chaudhuri has
shortcomings. Nissim Ezekiel, who is a great admirer of Chaudhuri, sums up his various drawbacks in the following words:

Snobbery, boastfulness, pedantic allusions, self-defensive coyness,
glorification of personal eccentricities, sly eroticism disguised as
aesthetics, and an over-ardent display of sensibility which has a
distinct *nouveau-riche* flavour—these are Mr. Chaudhuri's rather
formidable vices as a human being and writer. He hates everything
Indian and claims to have transcended the culture in which he was
born. The painful effort to do so has led him to personality distortions
of which he is blissfully unaware. This is not surprising in a satirist
but it is sad.[11]

Mr. Ezekiel, who is a leading poet himself, points out all the
major defects of Chaudhuri's personality. Chaudhuri was born
in India but he always believes that he is superior to all Indians.
He is very boastful about his Westernization. This pose of
superiority irritates many Indians who have the sensitivity of
Mr. Ezekiel.

The most brilliant critique of Chaudhuri has been written by
A. K. Majumdar, who is a leading historian in India. Mr.
Majumdar has exposed Chaudhuri's historical pretensions. Concerning Chaudhuri on history, Mr. Majumdar claims that he
has not only not read books written by Englishmen on Indian
history but "there is no indication in his works that he has read
books written by Indians."[12] Mr. Majumdar gives many instances
to show that Chaudhuri's version of Indian history is too gen-
eralized and superficial, and that it is meant only for foreign
export. Mr. Majumdar points out that Chaudhuri ironically

"has concentrated his efforts on knowing England while writing about India."[13]

Likewise, Chaudhuri knows much Latin and little Sanskrit. The reason for this is that Chaudhuri cares more for his Western than for his Indian readers. Mr. Majumdar gives many examples to show Chaudhuri's ignorance of Sanskrit. His lack of knowledge of the Indian classical language is accompanied by a certain deliberate distortion of the sense of compound words in Sanskrit. Mr. Majumdar rightly says: "The crude translations served Mr. Chaudhuri's purpose of presenting the Hindus as unrefined and crude."[14] Chaudhuri gives incorrect English translations because in a synthetic language like Sanskrit, it is easy to distort the idiomatic sense of Sanskrit compounds. Mr. Majumdar proves his thesis by comparing the bathetic translations of Chaudhuri with the refined renderings of A. B. Keith.[15] Chaudhuri's ignorance of Sanskrit makes one doubt the authenticity of his controversial statements expressed in *The Continent of Circe*.

Chaudhuri accuses his fellow Bengalis of envy,[16] but Mr. Majumdar has pointed out the most blunt truths about him. For instance, Mr. Majumdar says that Chaudhuri made many outrageous statements in his first book because the form of autobiography enabled him to dispense with evidence. It is for this reason that Chaudhuri's first work is an exercise in opportunism. When India attained independence, Chaudhuri started writing his autobiography so that he could please the retreating rulers. The British publishers accepted his lengthy book because the time was most propitious. Chaudhuri said in his book all those things which British fanatics would love to hear. Mr. Majumdar points out: "Mr. Chaudhuri not only depicted the past and present of the Hindus in general and Bengalis in particular in a manner most satisfactory to the British diehards, but also held out hopes for the future. Possibly more important was the fact that Mr. Chaudhuri absolved the British from all the criticism which Indians usually levelled against their Indian administration."[17] This is the main reason why an unknown Indian suddenly shot into the limelight. The early work of Chaudhuri makes one suspect that he put his brilliant English prose at the service of his English bosses.

S. Mokashi-Punekar is a bitter critic of many of Chaudhuri's

ideas. He says that very often Chaudhuri makes a mountain of
a molehill and that his work is full of fanciful generalizations.
Mr. Mokashi-Punekar further argues that Chaudhuri's method
shifts "ground from episode to generalisation, generalisation to
interpretation, interpretation to gossip,"[18] so that many of the
ideas look ridiculous.

M. Naimuddin Siddiqui makes an attempt to analyze the
nature and probable causes of Chaudhuri's alienation. According to Mr. Siddiqui, one cause of Chaudhuri's alienation is the
contrast between the England of his romantic imagination and
the India of disillusioning realities. In addition, Chaudhuri suffers from an innate racial and social snobbery. Another cause of
alienation is the fact that there is "an unsuccessful hybridisation
of the Indian and European culture in his upbringing."[19] The
other factors that lead to Chaudhuri's dissatisfaction with his
own country are skepticism, nonconformity, and maladjustment.
Chaudhuri has tended to use his alienation as an exportable
commodity for Western readers. Mr. Siddiqui points out: "With
a Diogenes-Thucydides-Narcissus complex . . . he resents the
'hostility' of Indian readers and critics, unaware of the fact that
his intellectual isolation is, in the final analysis, the cause, not
the result of his hostility."[20]

In "Nirad's Nightmare," Dilip Chitre provides a psychological
analysis of Chaudhuri's personality. He believes that Chaudhuri
suffers from schizophrenia and has a paranoid personality as
well. According to Mr. Chitre, "an acute sense of insecurity in
his own socity, a craving for status and acceptance, and a desire
to identify himself with the ruling elite culturally and emotionally, have all been decisive factors in Mr. Chaudhuri's
formulation of his views."[21] Mr. Chitre is also very critical of
Chaudhuri's grand style, prophetism, the insistence on creating
his own legend, and his grand theorizing. All this is caused by
an anxiety neurosis and the cognitive dissonance of a status-
seeking man.

II Style, Creativity and Scholarship

One may disagree with what Chaudhuri says, one cannot but
admire the way he says it. He is the most polished craftsman
among the Indo-Anglian writers. On his own admission, he

lavishes more care on his prose than most Indian writers do on their poetry. About his own hard work, he writes:

The Indian who writes English must acquire the technical mastery of the language, and this is very difficult to achieve. I am horrified to discover, when I have sent my books to the publisher after writing each page at least five times and sometimes even fifteen times over, that I have committed scores and scores of mistakes in grammar and idiom, and I go on sending corrections after corrections. This is very important, because the English reader and publisher will not regard any slips we Indians make as *slips*, but as evidence of our ignorance of the basic elements of their language.[22]

It is for this reason that Chaudhuri is very painstaking in his attitude toward English prose. He has been an ideal for other Indo-Anglian writers. He has not aspired to write slick English as some Bombay journalists do; rather, he wants to be judged by rigorous international standards. Hence he has taken great pains to write as well as the best English or American writers.

Chaudhuri's vast learning reveals itself in his writing. He is unusually fond of giving two ideas for one. Instead of saying that Indians write bad English because of the influence of their mother tongue, he says that it is so because of "the mutations caused by the linguistic genes." He does not put his ideas in simple terms. Instead, he always expresses himself in complex scholarly terms. Most of his terminology is borrowed from his wide reading of the natural sciences.

For instance, Chaudhuri has made good use of his knowledge of geology in all his books. In his autobiography, he explains our affiliation to the great movements of history in the following words: "In fact, I think the humbler we are the more completely are we made up of the material deposited by historical movements. . . . We are the sedimentary rocks formed out of these original igneous formations."[23] In his second book, Chaudhuri could never forget his life in India even when he was viewing the most beautiful sights in England. He mentioned this fact in the following terms: "I fear that in spite of my best efforts to decant the ratiocinative sediment some of it remains in the final product and cannot be separated."[24] In his latest work, he continues to use the geological metaphor. Thus, he writes: "I have arrived at a more adequate image for the German scholar-philosopher: he is the volcano which sends up hot, molten lava from his blazing depths, and that lava solidifies on the earth's surface to become the hard basalt of his books."[25]

Besides geology, Chaudhuri uses his knowledge of other sciences so that he can analogically explain his ideas. In these days, standards in university education in India are steadily going down. There is an ever-increasing rush of unqualified students because there is demand for degrees in every vocation. On the other hand, the economic value of university degrees and respect for university education are going down steadily. Chaudhuri explains this phenomenon by borrowing a metaphor from physiology. "In the twofold aspect of expansion and deterioration, atrophy and hypertrophy, the universities in India show a strange similarity to the diseased organs of the human body, say a liver or the thyroid glands, which grow bigger and bigger as they grow more inefficient."[26] In the same article, Chaudhuri uses another analogy from physics to explain the fact that the intellectual stature of a person in India is in direct proportion to the official position he occupies. In his characteristic way, Chaudhuri writes: "Generally speaking, official position in India is like a thermionic valve for intellectual reputation. If that position is high enough it can amplify infinitesimal intellectual input to hundred of watts of output, sometimes very distorted."[27] In this way, he enlivens his ideas intellectually by giving them the rigor of scientific knowledge.

Chaudhuri has made good use not only of his knowledge of science but of Western music also. He believes that Englishmen behaved unnaturally in India because they were in the confused chromatic scale. When they returned to England, they got back into their diatonic scale because their proper environment "effaced the accidentals and re-established the normal key."[28] In his latest book, Chaudhuri observes that Max Muller's life had the same unity which is to be observed in "harmonic and contrapuntal music."[29] In the same work, Chaudhuri uses another interesting musical metaphor. Marriage in the West has such a high frequency of divorce that it looks like a form of polygamy. Chaudhuri says that in this case, the notes are played *arpeggio* rather than as a simultaneously sounded chord.[30]

Chaudhuri is very fond of putting his scholarship on display. He tries to show that he has a good knowledge not only of many disciplines but also of some European languages. His style is flavored with bookish terms and French, Latin, and Sanskrit tags. Professor K. R. Srinivasa Iyengar has said: "His amazing scholarship no doubt gives ballast to the craft of his wayward sensibility, and the Latin tags, French quotations, German titles and Sanskrit citations sometimes introduce an element of the agreeably exotic and extraneous."[31] His learning is impressive, but occasionally it gives the impression of commercially attractive window-dressing. For instance, after expressing his disagreement with S. Radhakrishnan's interpretation of Acts 17:26, Chaudhuri writes:

St Paul simply meant to say that God had created the various nations of men out of one ancestor or substance (Adam or dust), and wished them to worship Him. Thus, in actual fact, what was uppermost in St Paul's mind was the diversity of mankind rather than its unity, except in worshipping one God. I went on to say that the word 'blood' in the A. V., which was probably responsible for the misunderstanding and which in Greek was *haimatos*, did not occur in the great Uncials, especially the Codex Vaticanus, and was to be found only in the Textus Receptus, the Codex Bezae, the group of Syriac MSS known as HLPS, and in the Peshitto version.[32]

The passage gives the impression that Chaudhuri is determined to put his entire Biblical scholarship on display.

As a stylist, Chaudhuri makes frequent use of too many literary devices. There are ubiquitous mythological references and Greek allusions. Thus, in his life of Muller, he records the fact that knowledge increases sorrow. This statement is followed by a flagrant display of antique learning. "Blameless Actaeon was torn by dogs for having inadvertently caught a glimpse of the bathing Artemis. The Artemis of life perhaps visits those who pry into her mysteries with the same punishment. Freud and Havelock Ellis, coming after Max Muller, seem to indicate that."[33]

To impress the lay reader, Chaudhuri makes an ornamental use of little-known books and historical incidents. His passionate and prophetic utterances remind one of the prose style of Nietzsche. Mr. Dilip Chitre remarks on this point "Mr. Chaud-

huri's impassioned rhetoric, whether he is writing eloquent praise
or launching a bitter invective against something, reminds one
of writers like Nietzsche. But the resemblance is deceptive although the pathological origin of the kind of prose does appear
identical. Nietzsche used literary and stylistic devices as heuristic
tools; Mr. Chaudhuri uses them primarily for their aesthetic
effect."[34] Because Chaudhuri employs a passionate and grand
style like Nietzsche, he appears like a Romantic historian and
religious prophet.

Occasionally, Chaudhuri makes too conscious a use of the
literary device. For instance, there is the deliberate use of
dramatic and traumatic contrast in the following sentences:
"My Western friends say that it [his house] reminds them of
the view of the Borghese Gardens from the Pincio. But after independence, for four years, I saw people easing themselves in
this park in the morning, sitting in rows."[35] His style shows his
split personality. Occasionally, it gives an impression of vacuity
because there is no correlation between the style and the content.
His pomposity and his egotism make him indulge in too-frequent
anecdote-riding and stylistic self-celebration. This appears over-
done when he deliberately displays his verbal pyrotechnics. The
following passage is characteristic of Chaudhuri's insulting
rhetoric: "I have recovered my Ariel's body from Sycorax, the
terrible and malevolent hag who stands behind Circe in India.
So I can and should ignore the Yahoos. But I would save the
fellow-beasts. They do not, however, listen to me. They honk,
neigh, bellow, bleat, or grunt, and scamper away to their scrub,
stable, byre, pen, and sty."[36] The last line shows how Chaudhuri
shows his vocabulary like a coquette displaying her cultivated
charms.

Chaudhuri's conscious pursuit of style makes him look decep-
tively like a creative writer. He is very fastidious in the construction of his sentences. He lavishes on them all possible
attention so that they can attain certain inevitable finality. He
makes deliberate contrast of the varying rhythms. As an instance
I quote the following sentences: "Scholarship is a matter of
temperament. Pattison had that, while Jowett did not. Jowett was
essentially and above all a pedagogue and a moralist. What
Jowett sought to do was to pour on to the three main interests

of nineteenth-century Englishmen, politics, money and religion, the spikenard of a refurbished Hellenism, which might be called Victorian neo-Platonism, but which was of course more superficial."[37] Such a passage appears obviously constructed for certain effect. Here, short staccato sentences are followed by a lengthy sentence which brings about the conclusion with a certain inevitability. Each sentence has the satisfying completeness of statement.

The wide range of vocabulary which Chaudhuri commands and the precision with which he uses it would flatter any writer of English. He has proved that language belongs to anyone willing to work hard with it and that patience and perseverance can overcome all environmental disabilities. In India, people still ask if creative literature can be written in English. By his impressive achievement, Chaudhuri has given the most fitting reply to that query. About his method, he writes: "My own practice is rather rigorous. After writing a book, I go very carefully over it, examining the diction and vocabulary, and if I find that I have used some fashionable words or jargon I weed them out, unless there is some special reason to keep them. As a rule, I remove all words which have not been good English for at least two hundred years. As I have found from experience, this pays."[38]

For Chaudhuri, what matters is not what he says but the way he says it. As long as he can provoke and surprise, he has fulfilled his own intention. He is very fond of making outrageous statements like this one: "The Hindu pantheon is as corrupt as the Indian administration."[39] On this account, he is a brilliant journalist, and most of his books are an exercise in extended journalism. His autobiography made such a profound impact because he made many astonishing statements. Although Chaudhuri was a passionate partisan in the Indian nationalist movement, he had no liking for the methods of Mahatma Gandhi. Thus, he described in provocative terms an unusual image of Gandhi as "a crude thaumaturge wandering with a following of Orphic mountebanks, the Coryphaeus of a pack of dancing dervishes or half-naked fakirs, for whom rationalised and civilized men could not feel anything but derision and contempt."[40] Thus, Chaudhuri impresses as much by his riotous mixing of metaphors as by his ability to challenge the most cherished convictions of his countrymen.

Chaudhuri went to England for the first time at the age of fifty-seven, but he has mastered the rhythms of English prose not by mixing with Englishmen but by making a conscious study of varied English rhythms. He has followed the advice he gave to other Indian writers: "It is enough to be familiar with the sound of English prose in the works of a fairly large number of authors of different ages and epochs."[41] But mere mastery of rhythms does not enable one to write brilliantly; what is also required is sincerity. Chaudhuri has written brilliantly when he has been deeply involved in his subject. Style is a matter of feeling also. Chaudhuri is at his best when he tries to convey some deeply felt experience. Thus, some of his major writing appears in Book IV of his autobiography and *To Live or Not to Live* where he is passionately involved in what he writes about and where he allows his subject to determine his expression. Few Indians have written as gracefully as he has done in some of his pages. But in Book IV of *A Passage to England,* he is as dull as his subject matter, and parts of *The Continent of Circe* look contrived and artificial.

Chaudhuri is remarkable for his craftsmanship, intensity of vision, and forcefulness of expression. From this point of view, he is the Flaubert and Walter Pater of Indo-Anglian literature. Through toil and tears, he has consciously evolved a style which is peculiarly his own. He is a dedicated scholar who has a native gift of grace in writing. However one may disagree with what Chaudhuri says, one cannot but admire the way he says it. Some of his outrageous utterances have made him the most popular writer in the West. But, because of his unique style, even in India, he commands admiration.

Notes and References

Chapter One

1. *The Intellectual in India* (Delhi, 1967), pp. 69–70.
2. I have borrowed this phrase from Chaudhuri's article "I Believe." He concludes this article with the following sentence: "If this faith has given me the strength and courage to work, love, and fight as I am doing at the age of seventy-two, when most fellow Hindus become semi-animate mummies, I can never be convinced that my faith is unfounded." *The Illustrated Weekly of India* (January 25, 1970), p. 31.
3. In a covering letter dated October 25, 1974, Chaudhuri wrote to me that his biography of Clive will be published by Barrie and Jenkins, London, in June 1975, while his book on Hinduism will be published in 1976.
4. The fourth stage in a Hindu's life when he retires to a peaceful retreat in his old age.
5. Robert Browning, "A Grammarian's Funeral," lines 83–84.
6. John Milton, *Samson Agonistes*.
7. *The Autobiography of an Unknown Indian* (London, 1951), p. 131.
8. *Ibid.*, p. 149.
9. *Ibid.*, p. 151.
10. *Ibid.*, p. 145.
11. *Ibid.*, p. 463.
12. *Ibid.*, p. 298.
13. *To Live or Not to Live, An Essay on Living Happily with Others* (Delhi, n.d.), pp. 149.
14. Samuel Johnson, "London, a Poem," lines 176–77.
15. *The Autobiography of an Unknown Indian*, p. 261.
16. *Ibid.*, p. 363.
17. *The Continent of Circe, An Essay on the People of India* (London, 1965), pp. 15–16.
18. *To Live or Not to Live*, p. 179.
19. *The Intellectual in India* (Delhi, 1967), p. 56.
20. *Ibid.*, pp. 54–55.
21. "An Iconoclast Amid Ruins," *Enlite* (Baroda, India, June 29, 1968), p. 30.

22. *The Autobiography of an Unknown Indian,* pp. 336–37.

23. *Khushwant Singh's India, A Mirror for Its Monsters and Monstrosities* (Bombay, 1969), p. 191.

24. "An Iconoclast Amid Ruins," p. 28.

25. Vijaya N. Shanker and Yash Paul Narula, "A man called Nirad Chaudhuri," *Imprint* (Bombay, September 1973), p. 16.

26. *Scholar Extraordinary, The Life of Max Muller* (Delhi, 1974), p. 148.

27. *The Statesman* (Calcutta, April 5, 1970), Magazine Section, p. I.

28. *The Autobiography of an Unknown Indian,* pp. 132–33.

29. In *The Bachelor of Arts,* Chandran and Malathi are not able to marry because their horoscopes do not match. In his other novel, *The Financial Expert,* R. K. Narayan shows the comic side of this faith in horoscopes. The hero of the novel, Margayya, bribes the astrologer so that his son can marry the daughter of a wealthy man.

30. *The Autobiography of an Unknown Indian,* p. 156.

31. *Ibid.,* p. 163.

32. *Ibid.,* p. 149.

33. *Ibid.,* p. 165.

34. The Abbé Dubois was a Christian missionary who visited India in the nineteenth century. In his *Hindu Manners, Customs and Ceremonies,* he presented a biased account of Hindu life. The third edition of the above work was published by Oxford University Press in 1906.

35. Katherine Mayo was the first American woman to describe India's dirt, disorder and squalor at length (in her *Mother India*). Mahatma Gandhi called her book "a drain inspector's report." *Mother India* was first published by Jonathan Cape, London, in 1927.

36. *Scholar Extraordinary,* p. 9.

37. *The Autobiography of an Unknown Indian,* p. 248.

38. *The Continent of Circe,* p. 226.

39. The whole incident is mentioned at length from p. 289 to p. 291 in *The Continent of Circe.*

40. *The Continent of Circe,* p. 290.

41. *To Live or Not to Live,* p. 9.

42. *The Continent of Circe,* p. 289. Chaudhuri's lengthy monologue is written on the previous page, p. 288.

43. *A Passage to England* (New York, 1966), p. 70.

44. Mr. S. Venkat Narayan mentions this fact in his article "Whatever's Happened to Nirad Chaudhuri" in *The Illustrated Weekly of India* (Bombay, November 26, 1972), p. 34.

45. *The Continent of Circe,* p. 18.

46. *SEE*, Illustrated Quarterly (Delhi, No. 11, October-December, 1970), p. 47.

47. Mrs. Mahindra's portrait is drawn by V. S. Naipaul in Chapter 4, entitled "Romancers," of his *An Area of Darkness* (Macmillan, New York, 1965).

48. Jawaharlal Nehru, *An Autobiography* (London, 1936), p. 597.

49. *The Autobiography of an Unknown Indian*, p. 470.

50. *Ibid.*, p. viii.

51. *Ibid.*, p. 262.

52. *Ibid.*, p. 514.

53. "Nirad Chaudhuri—A Study in Alienation," *Osmania Journal of English Studies* (Hyderabad, India, 1969), p. 45.

54. *The Autobiography of an Unknown Indian*, p. 514.

Chapter Two

1. Here and throughout this chapter, the number in parentheses refers to the page number of the *Autobiography*.

2. *Khushwant Singh's India* (Bombay, 1969), p. 190.

3. *The Intellectual in India*, p. 77.

4. *Critical Essays on Indian Writing in English Presented to Armando Menezes*, ed. M. K. Naik *et al* (Dharwar, India, 1968), p. 358.

5. *The Speaking Tree, A Study of Indian Culture and Society* (London, 1971), p. 383. Richard Lannoy's book is an outstanding contribution to Indology.

6. This point is fully developed in his article "Have We Forgotten the Mahatma?" in *The Illustrated Weekly of India* (July 26, 1959), pp. 11–13.

7. This article, published in *Survey* (London, April, 1968) provides an intellectual analysis of Indian nationalism.

8. *Survey* (London, April, 1968), 43.

9. *Ibid.*, 56.

10. Quoted in *Quest*, 57 (April-June, 1968), 71.

11. *Quest*, 57 (April-June, 1968), 71.

12. *What Is History*, Chapter I. Quoted in *Quest*, No. 57, p. 72.

13. *Quest*, 91 (September-October, 1974), 25.

14. This statement is made in *The Continent of Circe*, p. 174. Mr. Chaudhuri writes: "In spite of the currently held view, I have no hesitation in regarding the Zebu as a foreigner in India just as we Hindus also are."

15. *Quest*, 91 (September-October, 1974), 22.

Chapter Three

1. William Wordsworth, "Lines composed a few miles above Tintern Abbey," lines 27–28.

2. *Nirad C. Chaudhuri* (New Delhi, 1973), p. 43.

3. *The Indian Eye on English People* (Archibald Constable and Company, Westminster, 1893, pp. 38–39). It is interesting to note that unlike Chaudhuri, Malabari noticed many weak points in English character.

4. *London Magazine* (November, 1970), 69.

5. *Ibid.*, 74.

6. *London Magazine* (August-September, 1971), p. 74.

7. "Hindus Ignorant of Hinduism," *The Illustrated Weekly of India* (March 18, 1973), 27. Mr. Bharati goes on to add: ". . . the West smokes and fornicates only, the truly Indian abstains."

8. *The Autobiography of an Unknown Indian*, p. 450.

9. *Encounter* (September, 1967), 77.

10. *The Intellectual in India*, p. 77.

11. *The Times of India*, February 2, 1966, p. 6.

Chapter Four

1. *An Area of Darkness* (London, 1964), p. 70.

2. See, for instance, the scene wherein the hero, Krishna, whose wife has died recently, accompanies his mother to the bus station. An unknown lady asks his mother: "When is he going to marry again?" In spite of the objection, the intruder puts the same query again. The hero shouts: "When is the bus going to start?"

3. Particularly, his two novels, *The Untouchable* and *Coolie*, provide fine instances of social realism.

4. Chaudhuri's article "India's Kulturkampf" appeared in *Quest* (June-July, 1957). My review of Jhabvala's *A Backward Place*—published in *The Journal of Commonwealth Literature*, 3 (July, 1967)—elaborates the same theme.

5. *The Autobiography of an Unknown Indian*, p. 111.

6. I. A. Richards, *Basic in Teaching East and West* (London, 1935), p. 48: "Inability to consider meanings critically, lack of training in systematic comparison and discrimination, a tendency to accommodate a passage to a pre-formed view rather than to examine it for itself, these are not unknown any where."

7. "The Hindu World" in *Quest*, 61 (April-June 1969), 29.

8. Herbert Risley: *The People of India* (Delhi, 1915); second edition, ed. by W. Crooke, appeared in 1969. Risley formulates a similar classification of ethnic groups in the above-mentioned work.

9. *A Passage to England*, p. 103.

10. *The Crisis of India* (London, 1965), p. 153.

11. *Quest*, 91 (September-October, 1974), 23.

12. This literally means "religion." Here, it is used in the sense of doing one's duty.

13. "Indians and Chinese are brothers."

14. These two articles were written for two successive issues of *Quest*, Nos. 45 and 46 (Spring 1965 and Monsoon 1965, respectively).

15. *Quest*, 45 (Spring, 1965), 15.

16. "Three Myths about Indian Philosophy," *Quest*, 53 (Spring, 1967), 13.

17. *Vagartha*, 2 (July, 1973), 28.

18. *Banasthali Patrika*, 13 (July, 1969), 120.

19. *The Lotus and the Robot* (London, 1960), p. 136.

20. *New Statesman* (March 23, 1973), 422.

21. *A Passage to England*, p. 79.

22. *The Speaking Tree* (London, 1971), p. 65.

23. *Kama Kala* (Geneva, 1958), p. 34.

24. *The Times of India*, July 13, 1966, p. 6.

25. These references occur on the following pages: Shakespeare, p. 119; Milton, p. 80; Pope, p. 16; Coleridge, p. 300; and Kipling, p. 123.

26. *Hindu World* (2 volumes, London); quoted in G. C. Pande's review of the above-mentioned book in *Quest*, 61 (April-June 1969), 30.

27. *Quest*, 62 (July-September, 1969), 45.

Chapter Five

1. *The Autobiography of an Unknown Indian*, p. 390.

2. *Ibid.*, p. 391.

3. *Quest*, 71 (July-August, 1971), 93.

4. *The Autobiography of an Unknown Indian*, p. 69.

5. *The Illustrated Weekly of India*, September 7, 1969, p. 21.

6. *The Autobiography of an Unknown Indian*, p. 75.

7. *Ibid.*, p. 167.

8. *The Changing Status of the Working Woman in India* (Delhi, 1974), pp. 161–62.

9. *The Autobiography of an Unknown Indian*, p. 321.

10. *A Passage to England*, p. 120.

11. *The Hindustan Times* (December 29, 1968) p. 9.

Chapter Six

1. *Nirad C. Chaudhuri* (Delhi, 1973), p. 96.

2. *The Intellectual Between Tradition and Modernity: The Indian Situation* (The Hague, 1961), p. 119.

3. *The Illustrated Weekly of India,* November 9, 1958, p. 31.

4. *The Intellectual Between Tradition and Modernity: The Indian Situation,* p. 24.

5. *The Illustrated Weekly of India,* November 9, 1958, p. 31.

6. This is the specific word for the Indian Teacher.

7. *The Illustrated Weekly of India,* November 9, 1958, p. 31.

8. *The Intellectual Between Tradition and Modernity: The Indian Situation,* p. 50.

9. *Ibid.,* p. 14.

10. These two articles appeared in *The Times Literary Supplement,* September 27, 1974 and *The Illustrated Weekly of India,* March 11, 1973.

11. *The Times Literary Supplement,* September 27, 1974, p. 1029.

12. *The Illustrated Weekly of India,* March 11, 1973, p. 13.

Chapter Seven

1. Swami Vivekananda, *Collected Works,* Vol IV, Calcutta, 1963; quoted in *I Point to India—Selected Writings of Max Muller,* ed. Nanda Mookerjee (Bombay, 1970), p. 1.

2. *Life of Max Muller,* Vol. I and II (New York, 1902).

3. The two volumes of *Auld Lang Syne* were published in the years 1898 and 1899 respectively.

4. Muller's autobiography was posthumously published in 1901.

5. John Keats, "On First Looking into Chapman's Homer," lines 9–10.

6. W. H. Auden: "A Shilling Life," lines 7–8.

7. Nanda Mookerjee, ed., *I Point to India* (Bombay, 1970), p. 2.

8. *Ibid.,* p. 5.

9. *Ibid.,* p. 10.

10. *Ibid.,* p. 9.

11. *Quest,* 95 (May-June, 1975), 87.

12. *Quest,* 45 (Spring 1965), 15.

Chapter Eight

1. *The Autobiography of an Unknown Indian,* p. 217.

2. This information is based on a personal letter dated 25th October, 1974 which Chaudhuri wrote to me.

3. "The Fisherman" in *Collected Poems of W. B. Yeats* (London, 1961), p. 166:

> All day I'd looked in the face
> What I had hoped 't would be
> To write for my own race
> And the reality. . . .

4. *A Passage to England*, p. 95; Mr. Chaudhuri writes: "Every nation has its peculiar manner of self-projection, and since the climate limits our capacity for work anyway, we would be foolish to forego the advantage of talk."

5. *The London Magazine* (August-September, 1971), 74.

6. *The Continent of Circe*, p. 227.

7. *The Intellectual in India*, p. 46.

8. *The Times Literary Supplement*, December 27, 1974, p. 1463.

9. Chaudhuri thinks highly of his own articles. In a personal letter dated 25th October, 1974, he wrote to me that I should not write on him without consulting his important articles.

10. *Survey* (April, 1968), 53.

11. *Quest*, 71 (July-August, 1971), 49.

12. *Quest*, 91 (September-October, 1974), 22.

13. *Ibid.*, p. 23.

14. *Ibid.*, p. 24.

15. These comparative examples are given in A. K. Majumdar's article in *Quest*, 91 (September-October, 1974), 23–24.

16. *The Intellectual in India*, pp. 67–68: "Envy is more common and intense in India, and some Bengalis exhibit such a form of it that I have been compelled to recognise that they practise *Nishkama Irshya*, or disinterested envy."

17. *Quest*, 91 (September-October, 1974), 28–29.

18. *Vagartha*, (July, 1973), 30.

19. *Osmania Journal of English Studies* (Hyderabad, 1969), p. 42.

20. *Ibid.*, p. 47.

21. *Quest*, 62 (July-September, 1969), 45.

22. *The Intellectual in India*, p. 79.

23. *The Autobiography of an Unknown Indian*, p. 180.

24. *A Passage to England*, p. 3.

25. *Scholar Extraordinary*, p. 151.

26. *The Illustrated Weekly of India*, November 9, 1958, p. 30.

27. *Ibid.*, p. 31.

28. *A Passage to England*, p. 125.

29. *Scholar Extraordinary*, p. 48.

30. *Ibid.*, p. 148.

31. *Indian Writing in English*, 2nd ed. (Bombay, 1973), pp. 600–601.

32. *The Continent of Circe*, p. 288.

33. *Scholar Extraordinary*, p. 382.

34. *Quest*, 62 (July-September, 1969), 44.

35. *The Continent of Circe*, p. 31.

36. *Ibid.*, p. 309.

37. *Scholar Extraordinary*, pp. 213–14.
38. *The Intellectual in India*, pp. 78–79.
39. *The Autobiography of an Unknown Indian*, p. 450.
40. *Ibid.*, p. 401.
41. *The Intellectual in India*, p. 80.

Selected Bibliography

PRIMARY SOURCES

A. Books

The Autobiography of an Unknown Indian. London: Macmillan, 1951; Berkeley: University of California Press, 1969; Bombay: Jaico Publishing House, 1974.
A Passage to England. London: Macmillan, 1959; New York: St. Martin's Press, 1966.
The Continent of Circe: An Essay on the Peoples of India. London: Chatto and Windus, 1965; New York: Oxford University Press, 1966; Bombay: Jaico Publishing House, 1966.
To Live or Not to Live. Delhi: Orient Paperbacks, Hind Pocket Books, n.d.
The Intellectual in India. Delhi: Vir Publishing House, 1967.
Scholar Extraordinary: The Life of Professor the Rt. Hon. Friedrich Max Muller, P.C. London: Chatto and Windus, 1974; Delhi: Oxford University Press, 1974.

B. Articles

"Nationalism in India," *Survey*, 67 (April 1968), 41–56.
"Between Anarchy and Freedom," *Encounter*, XXIX, 3 (September 1967), 77–82.
"Tagore: The True and the False," *The Times Literary Supplement*, Friday, September 27, 1974, pp. 1029–31.
"From the Raj to Erotica," *New Statesman*, March 23, 1973, pp. 422–23.
"Indian England," *London Magazine*, X, 8 (November 1970), 66–74.
"Universal Darkness: Notes on the Decline and Fall of Indian Clothing," *London Magazine*, XI, 3 (August-September 1971), 64–65.
"India's Kulturkampf," *Quest*, II, 6 (June-July 1957), 11–25.
"Dichotomy in Hindu Life—I, II," *Quest*, 45 (Spring 1965), 10–16; *Quest*, 46 (1965), 20–28.
"The Language Issue," in *The Great Debate*. Ed. A. B. Shah, Bombay: Lalvani Publishing House, 1968, pp. 42–47.
"Are We Indians Religious?", *The Illustrated Weekly of India*, August 31, 1958, pp. 15–16.

"Indian Intellectuals," *The Illustrated Weekly of India*, November
    9, 1958, pp. 30–31.
"Have We Forgotten the Mahatma?", *The Illustrated Weekly of India*,
    July 26, 1959, pp. 11–13.
"Why I Hate Indians," *The Illustrated Weekly of India*. I: September
    7, 1969, pp. 18–21; II: September 14, 1969, pp. 14–17; III:
    September 21, 1969, pp. 14–17; IV: September 28, 1969, 14-17.
"I Believe," *The Illustrated Weekly of India*, January 25, 1970,
    pp. 24–31.
"Tagore and the Nobel Prize," *The Illustrated Weekly of India*, March
    11, 1973, pp. 6-17.

SECONDARY SOURCES

A. To date there is only one full-length study of Chaudhuri:

PAUL VERGHESE.   *Nirad C. Chaudhuri*.   New Delhi: Arnold-Heine-
    mann, 1973. Provides a useful summary of the first five books of
    Chaudhuri.

B. Articles

CHITRE, DILIP. "Nirad's Nightmare," *Quest*, 62 (July-September 1969),
    43–52. Critical account of *The Continent of Circe*; it tries to
    explain the work in psychological terms.
IYENGAR, K. R. SRINIVASA. *Indian Writing in English* (2nd ed.).
    Bombay: Asia Publishing House, 1973, pp. 590–601. Contains
    some useful comments on Chaudhuri's style.
KARNANI, CHETAN. "Nirad Chaudhuri and *The Continent of Circe*,"
    Quest, 57 (April-June 1968), 76–81. Material from this has been
    incorporated into Chapter 4 of this book.
KHUSHWANT SINGH. "Nirad C. Chaudhuri" in *Khushwant Singh's India*.
    Ed. Rahul Singh. Bombay: IBH Publishing Company, 1969,
    189–95. Intimate, personal account of the range of Chaudhuri's
    scholarship.
MAJUMDAR, A. K. "Portrait of an Indian Intellectual," *Quest*, 91
    (September-October 1974), 21–32. Pungent criticism by a pro-
    fessional historian of Chaudhuri's sweeping historical, philo-
    sophical and sociological generalizations about India.
MEENAKSHI PURI. "View from the Top," *Thought*, XXIII, 27 (July
    1971), 16. Discusses Chaudhuri's criticism of Indian society
    with special reference to *To Live or Not to Live*.
MOKASHI-PUNEKAR, S. "Nirad Chaudhuri—An Elegy on Liberal Educa-
    tion," *Vagartha*, 2 (July 1973), 24–27. Interesting article on
    Chaudhuri's method.

NAIMUDDIN SIDDIQUI, M. "Nirad Chaudhuri—A Study in Alienation," *Osmania Journal of English Studies*, VII, 1 (1969), 37–49. Brilliant analysis of the causes of Chaudhuri's dissatisfaction with India.

RADHAKRISHNA MURTY, L. "Nirad C. Chaudhuri," in *The Two-Fold Voice*. Ed. D. V. K. Raghavacharyulu. Guntur: Navodaya Publishers, 1971, 143–63. Discusses Chaudhuri's achievement as well as his affectation and pedantry.

RAGHAVENDRA RAO, K. "An Epitaph for the British Raj" in *Critical Essays on Indian Writing in English Presented to Armando Menezes*. Ed. M. K. Naik, *et al*. Dharwar: Karnatak University, 1967, 345–58. Full-length study of Indo-British encounter in Chaudhuri's autobiography.

RAJIVA, DEVA. "On Nirad Chaudhuri," *Quest*, 57 (April-June 1968), 69–75. Discusses at length Chaudhuri's theory of history, propounded in *The Autobiography of an Unknown Indian*.

RAMA MURTHY, V. "Nirad C. Chaudhuri and the Indian Psyche," *The Banasthali Patrika*, 13 (July 1969), 102–10. Critical analysis of the four Hindu loyalties propounded in *The Continent of Circe*.

RAMARATNAM, V. "An Inconoclast amid Ruins," *Enlite*, Baroda, Saturday, June 29, 1968, pp. 27–30. Brilliant account of Chaudhuri's diverse interests by his intimate friend.

STOKES, ERIC. "The Lesson of the Aryans," *The Times Literary Supplement*, No. 3, 799, December 27, 1974, p. 1463. Brilliant discussion of Chaudhuri's reputation in the West with special reference to *Scholar Extraordinary*.

VANMALI, RUKMINI, "Nirad C. Chaudhuri—Profile of ex-Colonial," *Socialist India*, VII, 14, August 25, 1973, pp. 7–8. Discusses the general Indian approach toward Chaudhuri's works and presents a useful analysis of his anglophilism.

VENKAT NARAYAN, S. "Whatever's Happened to Nirad Chaudhuri," *The Illustrated Weekly of India*, November 26, 1972, pp. 34–38. Intimate account of Chaudhuri's personal life.

Index

Acton, Lord, 39, 40
Alberuni, 37, 54, 62
Anand, M. R., 56, 67
Area of Darkness, 25
Arnold, Matthew, 46
Arya Samaj, 35

Babur, 54
Bach, 20
Beethoven, 20
Bharati, Agehananda, 49
Bhatkande, V. N., 35
Bose, S. C., 16
Brahmo Samaj, 34
Browning, Robert, 52-53
Bunsen, C. K. J. von, 100, 101
Burnouf, E., 101

Carr, E. H., 40
Chandrashekhar, S., 43, 90
Chatterjee, B. C., 35
Chaucer, 48
Chaudhuri, Nirad C.: birth, 14; influence of father, 15; influence of mother, 15; his education, 15; his jobs, 15-17; in military accounts department, 15; in *Modern Review,* 16; in All-India Radio, 16; in French Embassy, 17; his Bengali works, 20

WORKS—ARTICLES:
"Indian England," 47
"Aping the West," 53
"Dichotomy in Hindu Life," 62
"Why I Hate Indians," 77
"Our Unsocial Social Life," 84

WORKS—BOOKS:
The Autobiography of an Unknown Indian, 13, 26, 112, 113

A Passage to England, 13, 31, 109, 110, 114
The Continent of Circe, 13, 17, 23, 25, 52, 53, 72, 104, 114-15, 116
To Live or Not to Live, 14, 115
The Intellectual in India, 14, 115
Scholar Extraordinary, 14, 25, 115

Chitre, Dilip, 70, 120, 123
Churchill, Winston, 28
Collingwood, R. G., 40
Constable, 47
Croce, B., 40

Daji, Bhao, 105
Daya Krishna, 63
Deb, R. R., 105
Desani, G. V., 56
Deva, Rajiva, 40
Dubois, Abbe, 22, 62
Dutt, M. M., 32, 34

Euripides, 50
Ezekiel, Nissim, 69, 76, 109, 118

Flaubert, 126
Forster, E. M., 54, 61
Frost, Robert, 73
Fuller, J. C. F., 16

Gandhi, Mahatma, 23, 33, 37, 99, 125
Georgina, Beata, 104
Gibbon, 40
Goethe, 19
Grenfell, Georgina, 109

Hart, Liddel, 16
Haydn, Joseph, 100
Homer, 32

Iqbal, 87
Iyengar, K. R. S., 123

Jhabvala, R. P., 22, 56
Jinnah, M. A., 87
Johnson, Samuel, 17
Joshi, Anandibai, 105
Jowett, Benjamin, 99

Kalidasa, 50
Kane, P. V., 61
Kant, 102, 111
Kapur, Promilla, 80
Kaul, R. K., 65
Keats, John, 15, 47
Keith, A. B., 119
Khan, S. A., 87
Khorana, H. S., 43, 90
Khushwant Singh, 17, 19, 22, 29
Kipling, Rudyard, 54
Koestler, Arthur, 54, 65
Kripalani, J. B., 59

Lannoy, Richard, 37, 66
Lawrence, D. H., 69
Leibnitz, 19
Liszt, 100

Majumdar, A. K., 41, 42, 60, 118, 119
Malabari, Behramji, 105
Malabari, B. M., 46
Marx, Karl, 99
Mayo, Katherine, 22
McDougall, W., 74
Mehta, Ved, 44
Mendelsohn, 100
Menuhin, Yehudi, 101
Mill, J. S., 92
Milton, John, 32
Mitra, Rajendralal, 105
Mokashi-Punekar, S., 63, 119-20
Mommsen, 98
Moraes, Dom, 44
Mozart, 20, 100
Muller, Max, 34

Naipaul, V. S., 44, 54
Narayan, R. K., 21, 56
Narula, Yash Paul, 25
Nehru, Jawaharlal, 23, 25, 26, 29, 52, 60, 90, 99
Nietzsche, 111, 123, 124

Pande, G. C., 56
Pater, Walter, 126
Pattison, Mark, 99

Radhakrishnan, S., 24, 60, 90
Raja Rao, 56
Rajagopalachari, C., 57
Rao, K. R., 34
Ramabai, 105
Ramaratnam, V., 18, 20
Ravi Shankar, 101
Richards, I. A., 56
Risley, Herbert, 57
Rothenstein, 96
Roy, R. R., 34, 43, 87
Ruckert, F., 100

Saraswati, Dayanand, 34, 87, 101
Schumann, Robert, 100
Segal, Ronald, 54
Sen, K. C., 105
Sham Lal, 53
Shankar, V. N., 25
Shils, Edward, 85-86, 92, 94
Siddiqui, M. N., 27, 120
Stokes, Eric, 116

Tagore, Debendranath, 105
Tagore, Dwarkanath, 102, 105
Tagore, Rabindranath, 23, 24, 95-96, 99
Tilak, B. G., 107
Toynbee, Arnold, 115
Turner, 47

Valmiki, 32
Vatsyayan, 64
Verghese, C. P., 45, 85
Vidyasagar, I. C., 87

Vivekananda, Swami, 35, 43, 98   Wordsworth, William, 32, 47

Walker, Benjamin, 70   Yeats, W. B., 96, 113
Williams, Monier, 103
Wodehouse, P. G., 46   Zakir Hussain, 90

DATE DUE

2/Sept 84			